THE
BITTER THIRTIES
IN
QUÉBEC

THE
BITTER THIRTIES
IN
QUÉBEC

by Evelyn Dumas

translated from the French
by Arnold Bennett

BLACK ROSE BOOKS   Montréal

BLACK ROSE BOOKS LTD.

BLACK ROSE BOOKS NO. E 19

First Edition in French
"Dans le sommeil de nos os"

First Edition in English 1975

Hardcover — ISBN: 0-919618-53-7

Paperback — ISBN: 0-919618-54-5

Canadian Shared Cataloguing in Publication Data

Dumas, Evelyn, 1941–

   The bitter thirties in Québec / by Evelyn Dumas; translated from the French by Arnold Bennett. —

                          (Black Rose Books; no. E 19)

Translation of Dans le sommeil de nos os.
Includes bibliographical references.

1. Strikes and lockouts — Québec (Province)
I. Title.
HD5330.Q4D8413   331.89'297 14
ISBN: 0-919618-53-7; 0-919618-54-5 (pbk.)

Cover illustration: Rita Corbin

BLACK ROSE BOOKS LTD.
3934 rue St. Urbain
Montréal 131, Québec.

Printed and bound in Québec, Canada

land comrades

your name Québec like the blazing of comets
        in the sleep of our bones   like an intrusion of wind
        in the underbrush of our acts
here it is that earth's heart has already upset our furrows
        and our streets and our heart gives answer in the
        breaking up of old habits

PAUL CHAMBERLAND.

"L'afficheur hurle",
Éditions Parti Pris, 1965.

CONTENTS

preface to the english edition

As I reread this book almost five years after writing it, a few reactions come to mind. I will deal with the positive ones later. The main reaction is one of sadness, for not having been able to do a better job, and for not, so far, having seemed to give anyone the urge to push forward the research I was unable to pursue on an unsung period of Québec's labour struggles.

My second negative reaction is that I think there is an important methodological flaw in the essay, in that there was not enough wariness about the relative weight of the sources, both archives and interviews.

Still, there is joy in re-reading this book. I admit it. There is joy for having attracted attention to this particular period, largely forgotten or ignored, of labour struggles in Quebec. And because I am in love with the workers I met, in person or in imagination, I am pleased some homage is being rendered them through the book.

On a less emotional level, the subject matter of this book still gives me food for thought, for its own sake and for the light it throws on the period we are now living through in Québec. I will give a few examples in no particular order.

There is the role of immigrants, neither "Anglophone" nor "Francophone" — to use the accepted terminology — in the shaping of working-class struggles in Québec. The Middle European, Slav, Russian and paramountly Jewish contribution to the class struggle in the Québec milieu, on Québec terms, has not been talked about enough. Both Anglophones and Francophones, even on the Left, prefer to ignore it. But this sizeable category of people in Montréal factories or Abitibi mines cannot be forgotten. They constantly re-emerge, and recently, their support was felt for the Montreal Citizens' Movement, that strange agglomeration of opponents of the dictatorial Drapeau régime in Canada's largest city.

Another reflection that comes to mind about the 1935-1945 period is that Québec seems to have a knack for innovation in labour relations within North America. In the Thirties there was the law to authorize the extension of collective agreements to entire industries when a majority of employers and unions in the sector had agreed on a set of conditions. Despite its limitations, this system seems to remain the only feasible one for certain types of industries. The inspiration came from Europe, but was never followed in North America, except in Québec. Parallel to this is Québec legislation in the Sixties authorizing the unionisation of middle management. It seems this "marginal" part of North America, culturally and politically underdeveloped but with its eyes turned to the European experience, can best afford, of any part of North America, to try out new ways and means of social action.

This is true not only of what is granted (never without popular pressure) by official bodies and legislators, but primarily of some types of struggle. In the mid-Forties in Montréal, a city in transition (then as now), public service employees, including policemen and firemen, not only went on strike but also gained recognition of their unions. Moreover, as the provincial employees would do thirty-odd years later, they created a common front, each group of workers refusing to go back to work if justice were not done to the other groups of workers.

This all happened in Montréal or in the regions and industries where huge corporations (what we would now call multinationals) were implanted. It seems to me at this point that Québec opinion has paid to little attention to these factors. In my Epilogue, I challenged the Trudeau — Cité Libre view of things, but I now think that they are not the only culprits. The Québec intellectual mind seems to have a block when it comes to grasping the reality of Montréal and American capital. As a member of the

Parti Québécois — Québec's current political road to self-assertion — I actively hope that this blindness will be corrected.

For the struggles of Québec are those of the Chicanos, the Chileans and the Vietnamese, even if more muted: the struggle to be proud and free, against the American Empire.

Evelyn Dumas
March 1975, Montréal

preface

One evening at the end of a union convention seven or eight years ago, several of us were in a hotel room, drinking and smoking. Pat Burke, a miner of Irish origin who was then director of the Québec district of the United Steelworkers of America, was reminiscing about a miners' strike. As he recalled the assembly at the end of the strike, where he had to implore men who had struggled for six months to accept going back to work on the conditions proposed by the employer before the beginning of the conflict, this man who had lived through more than one difficult union struggle, this miner turned labour boss, had a tear in his eye.

That tear is the origin of this book.

It dawned on me then that what journalists (like myself) and other chroniclers retain of labour conflicts is superficial. The statistics, the reports on negotiations, the minutes of union meetings, are all nothing but an outline. From this realization was born an ardent desire to learn from the very lips of the principal actors in various conflicts in Québec history how they had lived these experiences, and to collect this testimony before it was too late, before these actors had sunk into death or oblivion.

For some years the desire remained a dream. Then I met the director of the McGill University Industrial Relations Centre, William A. Westley, and his active sympathy, his faithful support, allowed the dream to take shape. Although he cannot be held responsible for the weaknesses and deficiencies of the result, there would have been nothing without him. He obtained a research grant from the Canadian Department of Labour which served to finance the collection of data and the work of analysis.

Moreover, he never stopped believing that one day there would be a finished product, even when I no longer believed it myself.

The research was spread over two years, 1967 and 1968. As circumstances hadn't allowed me to push the investigations further, and since it seemed necessary to accumulate much more data, I had given up on writing a report. But friends made me realize that however imperfect my facts, they constituted new material which could help others, even if only as a point of departure for deeper research. Alain Pontaut and Yves Dubé of Editions Leméac showed interest. Journalist that I was, I needed only the deadline they offered me to force myself to write.

For the research itself I owe much to Clara Arsenault-Chicoine, to her rigorous intelligence and her enthusiasm for the subject. [1]

Here, in summary, are the references for this book: documents of the Canadian Department of Labour and other government bodies, interviews with witnesses to and participants in the period, and newspapers (general press and union press). [2]

Finding witnesses and participants for strikes which took place in Québec during the economic crisis of the Thirties and during the War turned out to be both easier and harder than had been at first foreseen.

In certain cases — and this is true especially where Communist and other militants whose organizations have been broken up are concerned — it was impossible to find the people whose names I had. In other cases, I knew where the people I was looking for were, but their relationships with the society around them had been profoundly modified with time, and memory was tinged with new perspectives that aging had brought. There was also the case of certain enterprises where employer-employee relations had remained bad enough to make confidences risky, even on such a relatively distant period. Finally, when witnesses could be found, they were most often union leaders, who had been leaders at the time of these conflicts and who had remained leaders afterwards. The ordinary striker is lost in anonymity and time.

It is to the anonymous striker, however, that this book is dedicated, to the striker of the Thirties and Forties whom history has never named, whom one systematically forgets by setting the postwar period, in many historiographies, as the date that the Québécois entered into industrial society and militant unionism. To this striker, carried along by the shattering wave of industrialization which marked the Second World War in Québec, tossed about by a society which was magical and almost monstrous because it was new and unknown, who was crushed in "the sleep of our bones".

FOOTNOTES:

1. She conducted most of the fifteen interviews with participants in the strikes, which make up the mainstay of the following account. She also did the work of a Benedictine by going through half the Labour Gazette, published by the Canadian Department of Labour, and finding each and every one of the strikes which took place in Québec between 1931 and 1945, with information on the demands, the duration, the number of workers involved, the result, etc. Finally she also did a part of the research on the newspaper accounts pertinent to those strikes which were retained as objects of description.

2. As far as government documents are concerned, I must stress the richness of the dossiers to be found in the archives of the Canadian Department of Labour, to which I had access thanks to the kindness of senior civil servants in the Department. Each strike which took place in the country since the beginning of the century has its own dossier, with press clippings (taken almost solely from English newspapers, it must be said), and, in certain cases, reports of civil servants. On consulting this treasure, I had a feeling of appreciation for the humble functionaries who for years took on the routine task of making up the dossier, in preparation for the day when this country's historians will for awhile leave aside political events, and especially the everlasting debates on the constitution and on national identity, to dig into the evolution of the Canadian and Québécois social fabric.

chapter one

the basic picture

This study covers the years 1934 to 1944. It was chosen because it is history yet at the same time relevant today. People who were young then are mature today, and their testimony can still be gathered. The events of the postwar period and the social upheaval of the Sixties in Québec have to some extent buried this period under calcified layers of memory, and few historical works have dealt with it, so that for the youth of the Seventies, it is as mysterious as the Middle Ages.

From 1931 to 1946 there were 667 strikes in Québec, affecting workers in Québec and in other provinces. [1] The climax came in 1942, when there were 133 strikes; in 1943 there were 103 strikes. Although there were more strikes in 1942 than in 1943, there were fewer large-scale strikes involving more than 1,000 workers.

The Québec economy was profoundly modified during the course of the period. The intense unemployment of the Depression gave way to the humming activity of the war period. In 1934, the number of wage earners (paid by the hour or by the piece, as opposed to salaried workers, paid by the week, the month or the year) in the Québec manufacturing industry was 152,502. [2] In 1939 the number was 180,448, an increase of scarcely 30,000 in five years.

But between 1939 and 1941, there was an increase of about 100,000 workers in this category. The number for 1941 was 276,415, and the curve rose until 1943, when the total reached 374,605, declining thereafter to 321,353 in 1945.

It is hard to imagine the impact on a society of such a sudden inflation in industrial employment. This was associated with an even more important jump in salaries, and in the general prosperity in which the ordinary citizen could share. In 1939, gross payments to wage workers in the manufacturing industry rose to $157,538,162. Two years later, this mass wage had almost doubled to $304,982,929, an increase greater than that in the number of workers.

The nature of the activities changed at the same time as their number. At the beginning of the period, in 1934, the textile sector was by far the most important employer (49,700 wage earners), followed by pulp and paper (28,234). The iron products sector was in fifth place, with only 16,184 workers.

All this began to change with the war. In 1943, for the first time since the appearance of manufacturing enterprises in Québec, the textile sector was no longer in first place. It was ousted by the iron products sector, which employed 108,085 wage earners while textiles only employed 76,202. The gap between the two categories in terms of salaries was even more striking: textile workers earned a total of $77,931,621, or about $1,000 each, in 1943, while iron workers received $204,357,222, for an average of $2,000 each.

In a parallel development, sectors that had previously been insignificant grew during the war at a staggering pace. The chemical industry, for example, employed only 5,823 wage earners in 1939, about the same number as the pulp and paper sector. By 1943 it employed 46,553 people. Employment in the non-ferrous metals sector increased from 8,255 in 1939 to 32,793 in 1943; it declined after that until 1945.

The tidal wave of war production clearly hit the Montréal religion the hardest, but it also spread to peripheral and isolated regions like that of Lac-Saint-Jean, where aluminum was produced for military aircraft. The industrial centres underwent a profound change and daily life turned in a new direction. It was not only the curfew, which nightly extinguished the sparkling circus of neon lights on Montréal's St. Catherine Street, that indicated to its citizens the coming of a new world. A sign like the sharp rise in users of public transportation, which enters the picture in the chapter dealing with the tramway strikes, also showed what a metamorphosis Montréal had undergone.

The period was also very lively from the political point of view: first there was the emergence of a third party, nationalist and reformist, the Action Libérale Nationale, followed by the creation of the Union Nationale, a party which would make its mark on thirty years of Québec life and whose anti-unionism was notorious; then came the War, with the debate over conscription, to which French-speaking Québécois were massively opposed, while in Ottawa, the War gave birth to a modern bureaucracy. All this coloured the social conflicts of the epoch. The political phenomena are dealt with in the following chapters only to the extent that they have a direct bearing on working class activity. But the facts are chronicled by historians, and better still perhaps, by a novel like *La Famille Plouffe*[3], by the Québec novelist Roger Lemelin, full of the flavour of the era in which industry, war, nationalism and religion mingled and clashed.

Labour legislation, and other forms of state intervention in labour relations, also underwent important changes between 1934 and 1944.[4] In 1934 the federal government had enacted only one piece of legislation, scarcely changed since the beginning of the century, providing for mechanisms of conciliation. In Québec, in 1934, the provincial government adopted a law providing for the extension of collective labour agreements, inspired by French and Belgian legislation. By ministerial degree, this allowed the extension of the agreements concluded between a representative group of employers and employees, to the whole of an industrial sector. This legislation, which is still part of Québec law, is unique in North America and was adopted following pressure exerted by the then Catholic unions.

Ten years later, in February 1944, the Québec government finally adopted a new set of laws, this time based on local conditions and on government reports that referred to them. These innovations had been in force in the United States since the first half of the Thirties as part of the New Deal which President F.D. Roosevelt offered his country. [5]

In 1937, the Union Nationale government of Maurice Duplessis adopted a law known as the Padlock Law, which barred access to all premises used for "Communist" propaganda, as well as all premises where "Communist" documents were found. The meaning of the word "Communist" was nowhere defined. This law was ruled unconstitutional, much later, by the Supreme Court, the highest judicial body in Canada. Meanwhile, it was used as an invisible bludgeon against union organizations considered by the authorities to be too militant.

At the Ottawa level, interventions in labour relations in the form of orders-in-council multiplied during the Second World War, culminating in 1944 (several days after the adoption of the new Québec legislation), with the adoption of P.C. 1003. This order-in-council gave Canada legislation similar to that which the United States had adopted a decade earlier.

In 1939, the Canadian Parliament modified the Criminal Code to forbid discrimination against union militants. In 1940, the Industrial Disputes Act (of 1907), which previously applied only to mines, transportation, communications and public utilities, was broadened to cover all enterprises related to war production.

In June 1940, the federal government called a meeting of union leaders to discuss wartime labour relations. The following year, in June, a three-number parliamentary commission was set up to judge disputes arising in sectors under federal jurisdiction. In September of the same year, it imposed an obligation on unions to have a vote among their members before declaring a strike. In October, it imposed a freeze on prices and salaries, and in December, through an order-in-council, it issued directives for commissions hearing parties involved in labour disputes. (In general, the salary level of 1929, before the Depression, was defined in these directives as acceptable for the war period.)

It was only after intense labour agitation and the publication of the report of a royal commission investigating labour relations, that Ottawa in 1944 proclaimed P.C. 1003, which, in particular, forced employers to recognize the union representing the majority of their employees and to negotiate with it.

Similarly the union movement underwent a metamorphosis during the decade between 1934 and 1944. At the beginning of this period, the "official" established unions were craft unions affiliated to the American Federation of Labour, with its many Canadian branches. The AFL was a form of unionism which developed at the end of the 19th century in the United States, in reaction to anarcho-syndicalist tendencies which manifested themselves there, as well as in Canada. [6] This unionism was distinguished by the privileged position which it offered to craft associations and to the most highly specialized workers. Among these workers it established lines of demarcation based on the distinctions between technical functions within a company. The AFL was "agnostic" in politics — it gave birth to Gomperism, named after its first president, Samuel Gompers, who preached that unions should support candidates who were "friends of labour", no matter what their party affiliation. This unionism was hardly attractive to non-specialized workers, particularly the assembly line workers, whose numerical importance was growing with industrial development.

In addition to craft unions, Québec had the Catholic unions, which were a poor relation of industrial unionism. Born after the First World War and rooted in "social Catholicism" with its corporatist tendencies, this unionism had its greatest impact outside Montréal, in the relatively weaker industrial sectors of Montréal, and generally in the sectors where Church institutions, as employers and as dispensers of construction contracts, could exert a direct influence. This unionism was conservative and believed in "cooperating" with management, in conformity with the Christian-inspired ideology that all men, bosses and employees, are brothers. It often had the support of French-speaking Québécois nationalists with reformist tendencies, and notably of the journalistic organ of this group, the daily *Le Devoir.* [7] Nevertheless, from the beginning of the period covered by this book, there were signs of change within the Catholic unions, change which had its origin among the most advanced elements of the Montréal region.

The enumeration of the official union organizations at the beginning of the period can end with a mention of the All-Canadian Congress of Labour, which grew out of the railroad workers' unions during the first decade of the century. The President of the Brotherhood of Railroad, Transport and General Workers, A. R. Mosher, was also the president of the Congress. This union central, more than the others, aimed at forms of industrial unionism, which brought together all workers in a factory, regardless of their trade, or even of their lack of a trade. It was also strongly committed politically, its leaders having been, in 1933, among the founders of the CCF (Co-operative Commonwealth Federation) a social democratic party based on the labour unions and farmers.

But there was also, at the beginning of the Thirties, a "deviant" and strongly militant wing in Canadian unionism, the Workers' Unity League, created in 1929 by the Communist Party (although not all of its members were Communists). Communism faced hostility everywhere because of the dominant ideology, yet Communist ideas fascinated a large number of North American radicals.

The WUL was deeply involved in several major labour conflicts during the first part of the Thirties, notably the Noranda strike and the first women's garment strike in Montréal. There is little trace of it that can be found today. In 1935 the political line of the Communist Party favoured common fronts, so the leadership of the WUL decided to disband it and integrate the militants into the infant movement of industrial unionism. This movement was created in the United States by the miners' leader, John L. Lewis, and in 1936 gave birth to the Congress of Industrial Organizations. [8]

The CIO made its first visible entry into Québec in the women's clothing sector in Montréal, through the International Ladies' Garment Workers' Union. This had long been affiliated to the American Federation of Labour before becoming one of the founding elements of the CIO. Taking its inspiration from the traditions of the AFL as well as from the new practices of the CIO, it was to some extent midway between the two.

The really new elements of the CIO penetrated Québec only at the beginning of the Forties, with the appearance of the SWOC (Steelworkers' Organizing Committee). They took root through the spread of units of the All-Canadian Congress of Labour, such as the Brotherhood of Railroad Workers, which implanted itself in the Montreal tramway system. The All-Canadian Congress, moreover, got together with units of the CIO to form the Canadian Congress of Labour, a rival to the Trades and Labour Congress which regrouped the unions affiliated to the APL.

The left-wing elements — communists, socialists or others — who had gathered around the Workers' Unity League at the beginning of the Thirties, in certain cases moved into the locals of the CIO. But sometimes they penetrated the AFL unions, pushed towards greater militancy under the pressure of the rising CIO.

Although at this stage the documents are inconclusive it seems that the social democratic leaders of the CIO, whose politics were more clearly defined than those of their competitors in the AFL, showed themselves to be more refractory, and even hostile, to the militants of the extreme left. It also appears, and again this is only a hypothesis, that the presence of the leftists explains the wave of strikes unleashed in 1942 by affiliates of the AFL, notably in the tobacco industry, munitions factories, pulp and paper, distilleries, and the shoe industry. The facts on these conflicts are difficult to find today, since the "purges" at the end of the Forties eliminated the Communist elements in the unions, and the ex-Communists who remain are very hesitant to raise the ghost of a "deviant" period in their past.

The Catholic unions, during this period, also changed. From 1935, despite the important reservations expressed by the top leaders of the movement, they showed bursts of militancy on the regional level: strikes in the shipyards of Sorel, and in Québec textile firms. [9]

The war would only accelerate the secularizing trend within the Catholic Union movement and would bring about a more spontaneous acceptance of a power struggle between opposed groups. Furthermore, since the Catholic unions had officers well versed in legal questions, who looked favourably on the labour courts of the war years, they appeared to be more effective than some of their rivals. The reorientation of Catholic unionism, the starting point of which is defined by several authorities as 1949, the year of the famous Asbestos strike, seems in fact to date back ten years earlier.

The revitalization of the established unions and the arrival of new elements, led to sharp inter-union struggles, which reached a climax around 1943, a year before the adoption of new legislation at the federal and provincial levels which defined the conditions for the official recognition of a union as the representative of the employees in a company.

It is against this background of abrupt transition from depression to prosperity, of epic political debates, of government war restrictions clashing with growing union militancy, and of the emergence of an industrial society in Québec, that the strikes of the period, in particular the twelve conflicts described in the following chapters, must be examined. [10]

FOOTNOTES:

1.

1931:	14	1939:	18
1932:	24	1940:	22
1933:	19	1941:	35
1934:	27	1942:	133
1935:	14	1943:	103
1936:	21	1944:	44
1937:	45	1945:	38
1938:	19	1946:	43

Figures taken from the *Labour Gazette,* 1932 to 1947.

2. Figures on employment taken from *L'Annuaire Statistique du Québec,* under the heading of "Principales statistiques des manufactures de la province, par groupes." The figures for each year appear in the edition of the following year.

3. ROGER LEMELIN, *La Famille Plouffe,* Cercle du Livre de France, collection Poche Canadien, Montréal, 1968.

4. Cf. H.A. LOGAN, *Trade Unions in Canada,* Macmillan of Canada, 1948, pp. 521-526, and JEAN-RÉAL CARDIN, *l'Influence du syndicalisme national catholique sur le droit syndical québécois,* Cahiers de l'Institut Social Populaire, No. 1, Juin 1957.

5. Cf. RICHARD O. BOYER & HERBERT M. MORAIS; *Labor's Untold Story,* Cameron Associates, New York, 1955, pp. 271 ff.

6. Cf. BOYER & MORAIS, op. cit., especially Chapter IV, "The Cross of Gold".

7. Between April 15 and May 7, 1919, the founder of *Le Devoir* set the tone in a series of articles later reproduced in a pamphlet entitled "Syndicats nationaux ou internationaux".

8. Cf. BOYER & MORAIS, op. cit., Chapter X, "Victory".

9. Cf. EN COLLABORATION, *En grève,* Les Éditions du Jour, Montréal, 1964.

10. See the appendix for the reasons which motivated this choice.

chapter two

the foreigners' strike

The northern mines attracted the unemployed like magnets. At the age of 24, L. left a small town in central Ontario to seek his fortune there.

"It was the Depression, you see," he said, "and people were looking for jobs, they were going here and there across the country, and in the north you knew that if you didn't find work in the mines or in construction, you could always find something to live on as a lumberjack."

He thus arrived in Noranda, with $5 in his pocket, one day in March 1930. It was a little frontier town, huddled around a copper mine, without paved streets or sidewalks. The forest was still nearby.

On that day, as on most other days, there were three to four hundred men at the gate of Noranda Mines, milling around, hoping they would be hired.

L. had in his pocket a letter of introduction to the mine superintendant from a Noranda merchant who came from the same small Ontario town as he did. He was hired.

"There couldn't have been more than ten per cent of the workers who were canadians, English or French. The great majority were immigrants."

The French Canadians called them "fros", a deformation of the English term "foreigners".

"One would have said that these companies, these big companies, throught that nobody could give them as good a day's work as the people from Europe," said L. "The foreigner, without a doubt, had a better chance of being hired than anyone else. They seemed to be looking for these big strong men from Europe. And the foreigners, they weren't like us, they didn't have a home outside of the mine, they came from very far away and they seemed to believe that they had to endure more, that they had to accept a bigger piece of hell from the bosses, to establish themselves here. In their situation they couldn't do otherwise."

L., as a miner, was paid 60 cents an hour for eight hours of work. The apprentice-miners received 53 cents, and the surface workers 43 cents. These were salaries that compared advantageously with those offered by the other mines of the region, even if they were cut by three cents an hour around 1931.

But the eight paid hours most often meant nine or even ten hours underground. The mine was still new, there were few pits, a single cage served to take the miners down at the beginning of the day and to haul them to the surface come evening.

One had to figure on thirty to ninety minutes for this transport operation. To make sure nevertheless that they got eight full hours of work, the company sent the miners down thirty minutes before the start of the work period, and at the end of eight hours the workers could wait as long as an hour and a half before returning to the surface.

Underground, "the conditions were much different than today," said L. "The ventilation left something to be desired because, since the mine was relatively new, they still hadn't dug all the shafts they wanted. There were more men underground than there are now, we didn't have modern equipment, and you still had to do much of the searching and cutting manually."

The miners came out of the pit with their clothing drenched with sweat and with the water that dripped in the subterranean galleries, and didn't have suitable locker rooms where they could change into city clothes. Either they had to share, with two other men, minuscule locker rooms where city clothes and work clothes were mixed together, or they had to go home in their work clothes.

"And going home in wet clothes wasn't funny," said L., "especially in winter when you had to cross the frozen, windswept lake on foot, because there wasn't any bus service then."

In January 1933 a first echo of the Noranda mine situation appeared in the *Worker* of Toronto, an organ of the Workers' Unity League, a completely Canadian, Communist-inspired Union which existed between 1929 and 1935.

Talking about the "nine to twelve hours paid as eight" that the miners had to work, about the five to six hundred unemployed in the "barracks" at Rouyn-Noranda, and about the "brutality of the bosses" who had, however, "built a church worth more than $80,000", the "labour correspondent" invited the workers of Noranda Mines to join a union.

L. said that the English and French Canadian workers scarcely knew about the birth of the Noranda local of the Mine Workers' Union of Canada, affiliated to the Workers' Unity League.

That is probably why thirty years later in Rouyn-Noranda one still refers to the peak of the 1934 organizing campaign as the "Fros'" strike.

"The day before the strike," explained L., "one indeed heard rumours that a delegation of miners had visited the general manager of the mine (H.L. Roscoe) to submit some demands to him, but either not everyone was informed, or it wasn't believed that this was really serious; in any case we were taken by surprise when we discovered the next morning on arriving at the gate to the mine that there was a strike."

In its June 23, 1934 edition, the *Worker* of Toronto gives a more detailed account of the events which led to open conflict.

Union organization began in July 1933. There were about 150 members at the start, but "due to the desertion of the then-functioning secretary and to lack of understanding of the tactics needed, there set in a period of stagnation in the recruiting of members."

Recruiting resumed in January 1934, following a six month plan established by the regional leadership of the union.

"Real shock brigadiers were found amongst the miners," wrote the correspondent of the *Worker*. "Some miners recruited over a hundred fellow workers into the union. During this time of recruiting, the union was functioning on a group basis. Group leaders also met on the various levels, in the shaft house, at the stations during meal hours, during changing of shifts, and at all other times when miners had the opportunity to discuss their grievances, even if only for a few minutes."

The same newspaper says that until April the union held meetings quite openly in the workers' hall in Rouyn. But L. affirms that he never had knowledge of such public meetings before the strike, that the meetings must rather have been held in another mining town, Kirkland Lake in Northern Ontario, or in the homes of the union leaders in Rouyn.

In any case, according to the *Worker*, from the month of April the union organizers had to be more discreet, because "company stools were getting in" to the meetings, and several leaders were fired.

To counter the company's actions, they formed a network of sections, whose leaders had contacts only with a few group leaders. In the spring, according to the *Worker*, the union numbered 500 members. There were in all some 1500 employees in the mine and the smelter at the time.

The union newspaper asserts that the "red bogey" was waved about to discourage the miners from joining the union, and that the shift bosses as well as the curés in the churches evoked the dangers of communism.

A reading of the spring 1934 issues of the *Rouyn-Noranda Press*, a weekly with pro-management tendencies, reveals numerous references to the Communist menace.

On June 10 the union held a public meeting where the members present declared themselves in favour of a strike if the company did not agree to a set of demands.

The next day, a union delegation met with the general manager of the mine, H.L. Roscoe, to present the following demands:

1 — Improved dry houses and a sufficiency of hot water for all; separate lockers for each man.

2 — Observance of the 8-hour day underground.

3 — Machine men's pay for runners.

4 — The right to join the union of one's choice, recognition of mine and smelter committees, reinstatement of five workers discriminated against for their activities in the union, and freedom from discrimination against anyone.

5 — Proper ventilation in the smelter against gas.

6 — 10 per cent increase in pay for all employees.

7 — Time and a half for overtime.

Mr. Roscoe does not seem to have received the union delegates very warmly.

"He was a jovial little man," said L., "always ready to laugh and joke with everybody. If you pressed him to the ground and threatened to choke him, he promised you whatever you wanted, but as soon as he got back up, he wouldn't give an inch of what you had asked for. He did all this in a very diplomatic manner."

According to the *Worker's* labour reporter, Mr. Roscoe told the union delegates that the company had prepared plans for a new dry-house two years earlier, that the improvement of the ventilation in the smelter had likewise been planned two years ago, that he "would have nothing to do with any kind of union, and especially not with the Mine Workers' Union which," he stated, "was only composed of a bunch of Communists", that the miners were getting high enough salaries and that in any case "the company could not afford to pay any more as there were 1,800 shareholders to split the profits."

And if the union delegates were not happy? "Go ahead and strike!"

The same evening, there was a new union meeting, where the members voted to strike. According to the *Montreal Gazette* and the *Ottawa Evening Journal* of June 12, about 300 workers attended this meeting.

On the morning of Tuesday, June 12, some one thousand persons, strikers and sympathizers, set up picket lines at the gateway to the mine. The activity of the smelter was considerably slowed down, but the strike especially affected the mine, which stopped completely that day.

Nevertheless, L. said that at noon, "It was already evident that the strike would be broken."

"The shift bosses went out by twos and threes in trucks and went around the town asking each man they saw in the street if he wanted work.

"Naturally, the people answered yes. They knew that the strike would be broken, and for the French Canadians it was their first chance to get into the mine en masse."

While the strike breakers were being hired, the forces of law and order were regrouping. On the 12th, one hundred volunteers, mostly company foremen, were sworn in as special agents by the municipal authorities. Sergeant Turnbull, commandant of the Provincial Police in Rouyn-Noranda, came back from Québec where he had been visiting to take command of the fourteen provincial policemen in the region. Reinforcements came as far as Senneterre by train, and then by plane to Rouyn. Hundreds of strikers and sympathizers assembled to watch the arrival of the three planes.

However, there was no rioting. The strikers distributed circulars and, according to the *Ottawa Evening Journal* of the 12th, "some rocks were thrown but there were no injuries."

The general manager of the mine declared to the press that 80 per cent of the workers remained loyal to the company and that the strike was the work of a group of communists with whom it would never negotiate. He added that the conditions about which the strikers were complaining were already being corrected.

The company maintained that the strikers only numbered three hundred (out of fifteen hundred employees), while the union claimed to have 950 members. A union leaflet said that the organization efforts in Rouyn-Noranda had been inspired by the successes of workers in other industries who, with the aid of the Workers' Unity League, "had obtained by their struggles better working conditions and salary increases." Two strikers were arrested for distributing the leaflet.

On the first day, the company hired a hundred men to replace the strikers, and the *Toronto Telegram* predicted that 150 additional men would be hired on the 13th. The unemployed rushed to profit from this sudden manna of jobs falling from the heavens.

The strikers and their sympathizers, at the gates of the mine, hooted and jeered at the new employees, whose qualifications were defined by the company as "experienced in mining work and in good physical shape."

The evening of the 12th, a crowd of about a thousand people massed near the Rouyn lake to hear the strike leaders explain the union demands. However, well to the south of Rouyn, the echoes of the event reached the readers of the Toronto and Montréal general press, and the Québec political authorities.

On the 13th, the second day of the strike, the provincial labour ministry wired the company directors with an offer to mediate. "When the union leaders are identified, we will make them the same offer," said Québec. The proposed mediator was Mr. Maxime Morin, King's Counsel.

The Ministry meanwhile ordered the closing of the liquor stores in Rouyn-Noranda. The picketers were pushed back from the main entrance of the mine, and miners as well as smelter workers began to return to work.

"I stayed out a day and a half," says L. "I really felt that it wasn't worth the trouble to stay out longer. The large majority of the English and French Canadian workers returned to work. The strikers stopped us at the gate, sifted us out, asking us why we weren't respecting the strike if we were members of the union...

"Among the picketers there were women with children, often with babies in carriages. This prevented there being any violence."

On the 14th, new police reinforcements were added to the already imposing number of guardians of the peace. Fifty additional special agents were sworn in, and thirteen provincial policemen and ten RCMP agents were on their way to Rouyn-Noranda.

There were two new arrests, bringing the total from the beginning of the strike to four, three of them for illegal distribution of leaflets and one for intimidation of non-strikers. Some men suspected of having made threats to non-strikers were detained by the police, without being formally charged.

An individual described by the metropolitan papers as being "a key man at the mine" was kidnapped, presumably by the strikers, taken twelve miles into the woods, gagged and abandoned. No arrest followed this abduction.

The union had opened canteens to feed strikers in need and their families. While the militants already seemed to be forming ranks for a long struggle, the metropolitan newspapers were announcing from June 15 on that the return to work was total and that the mine was operating at its normal pace.

The union newspaper would later denounce these reports by the "yellow press" and would assert that, on the contrary, the strike was effective except for some 150 strike breakers "paid $25 a day". It would even be said that the company was paying unemployed people 25 cents an hour just for walking the hundred paces to the entrance of the mine and showing how many people were ready to take the jobs of the strikers.

Calm no longer reigned in Rouyn-Noranda. Those who were working were escorted from their homes to work every day by truck.

The strikers tried to impede the circulation of these convoys by carpeting the streets of the town with nails to puncture the tires of the trucks. On June 16 the company counter-attacked: it brought out a steamroller equipped with a magnetic roller to go ahead of the convoys of workers and suck up the nails on the road.

The same day, the company said it was ready to rehire "all the non-Communists".

"There were plenty of inter-ethnic rivalries inside the mine and the smelter even before the strike," said L., "and they were let loose when the time came to rehire strikers. The team leader only had to say about a guy: that one's a Communist, and hop! the accused was eliminated. Personally I don't believe that the strikers were Communists, and certainly not all of the immigrants were Communists."

During the week-end of June 15 to 18, the strikers held several meetings, and despite the ban by the police, they called an open-air meeting which was halted by the rain. They launched appeals for help to union members in other regions and to the citizens of Rouyn-Noranda, asking for food and funds.

But by the beginning of the second week of the conflict, the company asserted its control over the situation. Taking the offensive, it declared what the newspapers called "a real lock-out against the instigators of the strike." The liquor stores reopened on Wednesday, and mass arrests of strikers and union militants began.

Before the end of the week of June 19, 34 strikers or sympathizers had been arrested. Union members in other regions of the country launched a campaign for their release. But in Québec, Liberal Premier Alexandre Taschereau declared that no "outside pressure" would stop the holding of the trials. Stressing that 33 of the 34 persons arrested in Noranda did not speak French, the Premier concluded that this proved his thesis that "outside agitators" were at work in the province.

Some of the accused went to trial immediately. Lloyd Nelson of the Canadian Labour Defence League, who had lived in the Rouyn-Noranda region for six years, was condemned to six months in prison for vagrancy. Twelve other persons, including three women, were found guilty of illegal assembly and fined.

If there were some union members in other regions who offered their support to the losing cause of the strikers, there were those, on the other hand, who did not hesitate to condemn them.

Thus the official organ of the Canadian Federation of Labour, the *Labor Leader* of Toronto, published a violent attack in its June 22, 1934 edition on the activities of the Workers' Unity League in Rouyn-Noranda under the headline "Reds invade the North".

The Canadian Federation of Labour, a short-lived organization, was a dissident and arch-conservative wing of the All-Canadian Congress of Labour. The latter was a completely Canadian union central which merged a few years later with the unions affiliated to the Congress of Industrial Organizations (CIO).

The CFL, which did not hesitate to introduce employer-dominated unions into places where other, more militant, unions had failed, assessed that the northern miners had nothing to complain about.

"In fact," said the *Labor Leader,* "Noranda in particular has always been marked by its just and equitable treatment of the miners. It is public knowledge that this company has always had a policy of lending any of its employees enough money to build himself a house if he wanted to establish himself permanently in the region. Furthermore, we are informed that the miners have free medical clinics at their disposal."

The newspaper added that Noranda's salaries were higher than those in American mines and it attributed political motives to the strike leaders: on the one hand, it said the dislocation brought about by a strike created conditions propitious to revolution, and on the other hand, the U.S.S.R. was often in competition with Canada on the world market in minerals and wood, whence the interest of a Communist union in injuring the production of these materials in Canada.

At the time that this attack by a rival labour body appeared, the Noranda strike, insofar as its effects on production were concerned, was over. But the judicial repercussions were not.

A first group of accused had rapidly seen their fate settled. A second group, of eighteen this time, appeared in Rouyn on July 7, sixteen of them charged with inciting to riot, and two charged with vagrancy. The judge set bail of $500 in cash or $1500 in property for their provisional release.

On July 10, a delegation from the Canadian Labour Defense League (a wing of the Workers' Unity League, and, like it, of Communist inspiration), visited Premier Taschereau to plead the case of those accused, and to ask that the bail be reduced. The principal spokesmen of the delegation were Robert Wright, secretary of the League, and Miss Beatrice Ferneyhough.

According to the *Montreal Gazette* of July 11, the Premier, who was also attorney general, declared that he could not intervene in the work of the judges, either to decide if an accused was guilty, or to fix the amount of bail. He promised, however, to see that all the accused who so desired and who had the right, could be tried before a jury. But he stressed that such an option could lead to long delays, and that there would not necessarily be release on bail in the meantime.

Mr. Taschereau seized the occasion to complain about "insulting" letters which he said he had received from people in Nova Scotia, Ontario, and even British Columbia, concerning the Noranda conflict, letters in which the provincial police were described as "strong-arm men".

Stressing that he would not give in to "outside pressure", the Premier declared: "Strike as much as you want, but peace and order must be maintained."

The delegation told the Premier and his Minister of Labour, Charles-Joseph Arcand, that the working conditions of the Noranda miners were very difficult, and that they often could not work more than five years because they were struck down by lung diseases due to the silica dust. They insisted on the right of the workers to form unions, to go on strike and to set up picket lines.

Messrs. Taschereau and Arcand conceded the legitimacy of these three rights, but the Labour Minister declared that, as a member of an international union, he had participated in picket lines, and that he had always understood that they had the aim of stopping members of the union from working during the strike but not of putting pressure on other citizens.

Finally, the Premier invited the unionists to consult the Minister of Labour more often, and especially whenever there was a question of starting a strike.

Meanwhile, in Noranda, life had resumed its course. On July 26, the *Rouyn Noranda Press* made known an important change in the composition of the labour force which had followed the strike.

Under the heading "Inestimable service is rendered by the Reds — Canadians now greatly in majority", the newspaper declared that as a result of the strike the percentage of foreign-born workers employed in the mine had fallen from 50 to 25 per cent of the manpower, and that the proportion of French-Canadian workers had considerably increased.

The newspaper said that on June 11, before the strike, there were only 188 French-Canadian workers at the Noranda mine. On July 1 there were 450.

As for the English Canadians, their number went up from 416, or 27 per cent of the manpower before the strike, to 544, or 35 per cent of the Manpower on July 1.

The (foreign-born) naturalized Canadian citizens were 354 in number before the strike; now they were only 195.

Finally, with respect to foreigners who had not obtained Canadian citizenship, the newspaper gave the following information, furnished by the general manager of the mine, H.L. Roscoe: Yugoslavs were 149 before the strike, 43 after; Czechoslovaks went from 39 to 17; Ukrainians, Poles and Russians from 91 to 54; Austrians from 10 to 4; Serbs from 5 to 2; Finns from 35 to 9; Swedes from 15 to 7. There was little change with respect to the relatively small number of Hungarians,

Roumanians, Bulgars, Italians, Norwegians, Danes, Montenegrins, Belgians, Swiss, Germans, French and Dutch.

"Of course," comments the *Rouyn Noranda Press,* "the nature of the service involuntarily rendered by the Communists was that by their action in bringing about the strike, they forced attention upon the growing menace of the increasing percentage of foreign workers employed in our mining centres, to which, sooner or later, a halt had to be called if our own people were to be assured of a square deal. Noranda Mines Limited went right to the root of the matter when it refused to take back foreign agitators who instigated the strike, and replaced them by loyal Canadians, and it is to be hoped that the preponderance of our own people on the Company payroll will continue to be maintained."

These "foreigners", these "fros", now came to know what the Premier had promised them — "British justice". In company with other workers arrested following a lumberjacks' strike in the same region, they went on trial at the beginning of December 1934. In condemning them, Judge Roméo Langlais of Québec admonished the accused, describing them as "foreigners" and "troublemakers" who "would bitterly regret their actions".

The following men were condemned to two years in the penitentiary and to deportation for having provoked a riot: Nick Skubin, L. Loreskevich, Tony Busich, John Shulentich, Frank Dukovac, T. Majerle, Matt. Persil, A. Rehikainen, Mike Punkiak, John Nishila, John Balkovich, Karl Bacich, Tony Cludmovitch, George Ewaniuk and L. Shuster.

In addition, J. Martinch was condemned to six months in the penitentiary for participating in an illegal assembly and Harry Raketti to eighteen months for sedition. Raketti was released a little afterwards because he was seriously ill.

The Canadian Labour Defense League had retained the services of a lawyer, Mr. Michael Garber, to defend the accused and to appeal against their condemnation. During the appeal, release on bail was refused and the

Court of Appeal, in confirming the lower court judgement, decreed that the time spent in prison while awaiting the result of the appeal would not count towards the completion of the sentence.

The League then pursued its campaign to obtain the release of the prisoners and to have the deportation sentences lifted. It received support in this campaign from personalities such as P.M. Draper, of the Trades and Labour Congress of Canada, J.S. Woodsworth, national leader of the social-democratic party (CCF), Mr. Blackmore, of the Social Credit party, and the federal M.P., H.H. Stevens.

While the condemned served their sentences, the WUL made a new attempt at union organization in Noranda in April 1936. There were twelve immediate firings for union activities, and according to the organ of the WUL, the *Worker,* 70 other workers were threatened with firing. The same paper, asserting that it was French Canadians who "broke the strike" of 1934, said that they were now the first to hope for the formation of a union. But this new organizing attempt did not last long.

Finally, on the last day of June 1936, fifteen of those condemned in the Noranda strike were released from Bordeaux Jail. There were no more than two still affected by a threat of deportation, to Yugoslavia—Matt. Persil and John Sulentich.

The sympathizers who had struggled to obtain their liberty wanted to give them a party in Montréal. But the released prisoners had been given train tickets to the north valid for only one day. To those who had supported them during their captivity they addressed the following collective message:

"We express our enthusiastic recognition to the Canadian people for the struggle which it waged in our name. We promise to immediately resume our place in the class struggle."

Where did they go then? It is impossible to pick up their trail today, or even to know if the last two men condemned to deportation were really deported.

In Noranda, relative calm reigned. A company committee tolerated by the boss spoke in the name of the workers for a while. But ten years went by before other workers took up the cause of the "fros", led other struggles and began other strikes for union recognition.

chapter three

the shmata strikes

"On parle un peu partout
De stars de cinéma,
Mais nous avons chez nous
Ici au Canada
De jolies midinettes
Au charme sans pareil
Qui de leurs doigts de fées
Nous offrent des merveilles."
(Les midinettes, union song)

(Almost everywhere they're talking
About stars of the cinema,
But we have right here,
Here in Canada,
Pretty working girls
With unequalled charm
Who with their fairy-like fingers
Present us with wonders.)

(The Working Girls — translation of union song.)

In Montréal the garment industry — or the "rag trade" or "shmata business" as one used to say at that time — was shaken by many labour conflicts during the Thirties. From 1934 to 1940, scarcely a month went by without the *Labour Gazette,* a federal government publication, having some strike to report in one sector or another — in men's clothing, women's clothing, millinery, or furs.

All sectors were hit, but there was one, dress-making, where the conflicts were more spectacular than elsewhere. The large majority of workers in this sector were women. Two types of unionism appeared on the scene, and confronted each other in a conflict which finally led to the defeat of one type by the other, while in the background a third union maneuvered, sometimes ambiguously.

The strikes in the dress industry, more than in any other sector, affected large numbers of workers, men and women: 45,000 man-days were lost in a single conflict in 1934, and 55,000 in 1937.

One of the two unions which emerged and engaged in a fight to the death in the dress industry was the International Ladies' Garment Workers' Union, which was first affiliated to the American Federation of Labour but which later participated in the founding of the Congress of Industrial Organizations. The other was the Needle Workers' Industrial Union, affiliated to the Workers' Unity League, a Canadian Communist-inspired union which existed for only six years before disbanding in 1935.

In the background was the Canadian and Catholic Confederation of Labour, which conservative elements of the clergy and certain employers tried to use for a while to counter the organizing efforts of "neutral" and "communist" unions.

There are also two men whose names will forever be entangled in this epic: Bernard Shane, of the International Ladies' Garment Workers' Union, and Joshua Gershman, secretary general of the Needle Workers' Industrial Union.

Although it was one of the principal sources of employment in Montréal during these years of economic crisis, the industry was far from being solidly established. On the flanks of a few "big" companies, tens and hundreds of little ones swarmed, often set up by ex-workers who first hired brothers, sisters and cousins, resisting for better or worse and more often for worse the shrinking of the market due to the depression and to the seasonal fluctuations characteristic of the industry. Bankruptcies abounded and few enterprises survived ten years.

In the face of growing unionization the bosses formed their own associations. In the beginning the majority of bosses and workers were Jews, and it was only in the second half of the decade that the French-Canadian presence made itself strongly felt, particularly in dressmaking. Later, after the Second World War, recruits from each new wave of immigrants would come to add themselves to the French-Canadian working girls: Italians, Greeks, Portuguese. But the militancy of the Jews who had fled the pogroms of Europe and then the fascist persecution was a determining factor in the building of the garment unions, in Montréal as in the other centres of the garment industry in North America (New York, Chicago, Winnipeg and Toronto especially).

Joshua Gershman's father, a Ukrainian merchant, had immigrated to Canada in 1913, fleeing the pogroms. Joshua followed him in 1921—he was 19 years old—and settled in Winnipeg.

In Russia, while pursuing studies in a Jewish theological seminary, Joshua had become interested in Marxism and had associated with a group of young revolutionaries in his native city. He passionately supported the Russian revolution. When he landed in Canada he was already, in his own words, "won to the labour cause", and he threw himself into the union struggle from the moment of his arrival in Winnipeg.

At 24 he was one of the leaders of the first general strike of the fur workers in Winnipeg. After the strike he could no longer find a job anywhere in the city, presumably because the employers had decided to get rid of him. He went to Toronto, where he again associated with revolutionary movements. "But the Winnipeg bosses found out where I was," he said. "They warned the Toronto bosses and soon I couldn't find work there either." In 1927 he went to New York to work as a journalist on *Freiheit,* a leftist daily. Two years later, his comrades in the Communist movement recalled him to

Toronto and asked him to work as an organizer for the Needle Workers' Industrial Union, of which he became secretary general in 1930.

In that year he came to Montréal for the first time. Afterwards, although he went back and forth between Montréal and Toronto, he spent the largest part of his time in Montréal, getting the union message into one shop after another.

The garment cutters, indispensible to the industry, were the first and easiest workers to unionize. If they stopped working, the whole business was paralyzed. There were numerous cutters' strikes in the early Thirties in Montréal. These aristocrats of the industry were not always affiliated to the Needle Workers' Industrial Union but they often supported its actions.

The most difficult to convince were the young girls, particularly the French Canadians. A story is told that once, in one shop, cutters and pressers demanded that the semi- and non-specialized workers, the drapers and finishers, be given a salary increase comparable to that which they had won. So the girls won a raise of $2.50 a week, which was given to them Friday, after two days on strike. On Monday six girls showed up in the union office and explained to the union representative that they wanted to give him their $2.50 increase "because we went to church yesterday and it was explained to us that this money was a sin, that it was a sin to accept it." The union representative had to visit the parents of these girls to tell them that if a sin was being committed, it was the bosses who were committing it by offering salaries of $9, $10 and $12 a week.

In early 1934, at the third national convention of the Needle Workers' Industrial Union, it was decided that this year there would be two general strikes in the dress industry, one in Toronto and one in Montréal. (The Toronto strike took place at the beginning of the summer).

The brief, one-shop strikes which had broken out regularly during the four preceding years, had prepared the ground for the general strike in Montréal. The workers, encouraged by the frequent successes of their tradesman colleagues, also wanted to better their lot.

And the working conditions in that period, all the evidence shows, were extremely difficult.

The salaries were low. The minimum wage law set a floor for the payment of women (and of women only) but the legislation was constantly violated. A worker could receive as little as $5 or $6 for a 70-hour week. To evade state prosecution, certain employers forced two and sometimes three women from the same family to punch the same attendance card, so that a single salary was paid for the work of two or three people.

But low salaries and long hours of work were not the only grievances. Poor hygiene prevailed in many of the shops. Under feeble lighting, squeezed in along big tables, the male and female workers often worked in company with cockroaches and other pests, suffocating from the heat during the summer months.

A system of favouritism reigned in more than one shop. The sister, the cousin or the mistress of the foreman was assured of a steady job; the others weren't. Sometimes big or petty bosses required a working girl to bestow her favours on them before they gave her the package of cut pieces with which she would sew a dress or a blouse for a few cents.

A working woman of the period recounts that one day, when her fortune was reduced to ten cents and she didn't have any more money either for her rent or for her food, she and ten others were waiting for work in a shop. The foreman arrived with a package which, once finished, would have been worth $100. Instead of dividing it among the ten women who were trying to earn a living, he gave the whole package to his favourite, despite the entreaties of the others.

One can be Catholic and tremble on Sunday when the curé preaches against the Communist menace, but a time comes when such conditions become unbearable.

One event finally convinced the majority of the working girls of the need for a union. The International Ladies' Garment Workers' Union — which they subsequently joined — had unleashed a strike of the coat cutters in March. In July, after its success in this limited sector, it used the threat of a strike to obtain improved conditions for non-specialized working women in the coat-making sector.

The speeches of Joshua Gershman and his associates no longer fell on deaf ears. The bosses also began to take the unions seriously. Faced with the strikes of early 1934 and the agitation which they could not miss seeing in the dress-making sector, they formed their own association.

On August 21, 1934, in the Auditorium Hall on Ontario Street West, a crowd of working men and women, encouraged by the Needle Workers' Industrial Union, decided to engage in a general strike in the dress-making industry.

The workers called for increases to raise salaries to a minimum of $12.50 a week for finishers and $30 for cutters, a 44-hour week, the abolition of penalty clauses and the recognition of their union.

The next day some 4,000 working men and women were in the street, and about 125 shops along Bleury, St. Catherine and Peel Streets—the garment district— were paralyzed.

Never had so many women demonstrated in Montréal. The numerous policemen guarding the doors of the establishments showed themselves to be rather sympathetic to these unexpected picketers, whom they regarded as pretty girls. Moreover, eyewitnesses say that the police were sympathetic to the strikers because often members of their family were among them, and even the police knew how difficult it was to live on the low salaries of the Depression years.

The Needle Workers' Industrial Union could count on about 120 leaders, delegates from shops and officials of the local, to organize the strikers' action. It was they who, several weeks before the strike, had held preparatory meetings. It was they who, at five in the morning the day the strike began, met at the union headquarters and went out with leaflets announcing to the workers that the strike was starting that day. Some of them got into the shops, seized the telephones to stop the bosses from calling the police, and shut off the electricity, stopping the machines.

Large numbers of picketers massed in front of the shops each morning between seven and eight-thirty. The first incidents broke out on the second day of the strike, and three young people were arrested for trying to shut off the power in a shop where the work was going on despite the strike.

The Montréal cutters' union, which was not affiliated with any other organization. became the first object of management advances. During the strike, the management association negotiated only with this union, and refused to continue these negotiations when the cutters made a common front with the Needle Workers' Industrial Union.

On August 27 the Montréal daily, *The Herald,* headlined that "American goons invade Montréal to break the strike" and reported that strikers marching through the garment district were attacked by "a group of men armed with bludgeons, lead pipes and rubber hoses filled with sand".

Municipal and provincial police on horseback dispersed the crowd with whip handles. An eye-witness reports that the young girls defended themselves from the police charges by sticking pins in the horses' flesh.

On the 28th, during a strikers' assembly at the Auditorium, an outburst at the back of the hall created a panic and a crowd of workers went out to demonstrate in front of two big garment factories, blocking traffic on St. Catherine Street, which was and still is an important artery. The public authorities spoke of a riot, and there were twelve arrests: ten women and two men.

That same day the Minister of Labour, Charles-Joseph Arcand, proposed to the bosses and the strikers that they submit their dispute to arbitration by a third party.

On April 20, 1934, the Minister had the legislature adopt a "law relating to the juridical extension of collective labour agreements", known as the "Arcand law", which allowed the extension by decree to a whole industry of the agreements concluded between a representative number of employers and unionists. The Catholic unions had been calling for this measure for several years. To benefit from it, however, the unions first had to conclude an agreement with the bosses, and this was even more difficult since nothing in that era forced the employers to negotiate with the representatives of their employees. The Labour Minister urged arbitration as the missing key to his system of industrial relations.

The offer of arbitration was immediately accepted by the bosses, but the union rejected it. "Who is the Minister of Labour?" the strike leaders declared to the press.

Thirty years later many commentators would say that this rejection of arbitration was due to the Communist and revolutionary tendencies of the leaders of the Needle Workers' Industrial Union, and that it produced a clear and abrupt negative change in the attitude of the public and of the strikers themselves to the strike.

But the union leaders asserted that arbitration had been applied to other conflicts which had broken out earlier in the same year, and that invariably the arbitrator favoured the management position.

The strike did not abate with the rejection of arbitration. On August 29 the union offices were ransacked by goons. A union delegation visited the Montréal police chief, Fernand Dufresne, who according to the newpapers "gave them the right" to set up their picket lines in front of the 90 establishments involved in the conflict, and invited them to obtain summonses against anyone who attacked the strikers.

On August 29 the Minimum Wage Commission, a provincial government board, had revised the salary rates of women working in the garment industry. It had decreed that the employers had to hire 70 per cent of specialized working women at $12.50 for a week reduced from 55 to 48 hours.

On announcing his decision, the president of the Commission, Gustav Francq, admonished the employers:

"It is a disgrace," he said. "I have brought almost every one of you, one by one, before the courts of justice to make you pay the minimum wage. I have hauled more firms into court from the dress-making sector than from any other sector. I do not know of another industry which allows such flagrant violations of the law. This is perhaps due to the fact that you are always in a hurry to open a shop with only a few dollars in your pocket."

The commission fixed the salary rates of non-specialized beginners at $7 per week, which had to be raised to $8 after six months, $9.50 after 12 months, $11 after 18 months and $12.50 after 24 months.

In early September, people started to talk about a settlement. The accounts were contradictory: the union said that 23 establishments out of 90 had concluded agreements, while the management association asserted that no agreement had been reached.

A few days later the employers accused the union of being dominated by the Communists, and said that it was for that reason that they refused to negotiate with it. Two bosses, speaking for the others, declared to the *Herald* that they were thinking of moving their businesses, but not to Toronto "because the radicals control the industry in that city. We would be going out of the frying pan into the fire. We are presently examining the possibilities in the suburbs in order to prepare for the future."

On September 11, the daily *Gazette* predicted that the strike would be completely over within a few days, after the Jewish holidays. The employers, through one of their spokesmen, affirmed that there was dissension within the union and that only about twenty small establishments—of which none was a member of the management association—had concluded agreements.

The next day one of the union leaders confirmed that there were agreements in 25 firms, and added that the strike was continuing in 25 others. None of the agreements provided for the recognition of the union.

According to a report to the federal Minister of Labour from his representative in Montréal, the strike was effective for two weeks, but was not officially declared over before October 12.

However, the organ of the Workers' Unity League, the *Worker,* said on September 29 that the dressmakers in Montréal were seeking to consolidate their union by returning to work, and published a letter signed by the strike committee which, to all intents and purposes, recognized the defeat of the union.

This same letter stressed that the strike had given proof of a militancy which was supposed to be nonexistent among French-Canadian workers, and maintained that the wave of militancy in Québec had pushed government and management to "teach a lesson", through the workers of the dress industry, to all the French-Canadian workers.

"The question of arbitration, pushed by Mr. Arcand, was only another attempt on the part of the provincial authorities to break the powerful mass strike of the dress workers and leave them to the mercy of a so-called impartial committee whose judgment in all cases favours the bosses," said the *Worker.* "The arbitration in the case of the railwaymen, the Vancouver dockers and the Montréal cutters proves our thesis."

The Needle Workers' Industrial Union, according to good Communist tradition, also criticized itself in this article.

"Here are the weaknesses of our union, which showed up glaringly during the strike battles: the leadership did not have a broad enough base, the problems were not sufficiently aired as they came up, we neglected to prepare each striker for active, conscious and creative work, we neglected to fight all the provocations, slanders and lies of the manufacturers and of the capitalist press as well as the machinations of the agents of the employers among the strikers."

In any event, according to the report of the representative of the Minister of Labour, the results of the strike were the following: The majority of the 90 establishments affected gave salary increases of about 20 per cent. Only some firms recognized the union, however.

Of the 90 establishments, 35 did not conclude any agreement, and the others made verbal agreements.

The report goes on to say that the main spokesman of the management association declared the union "broken"; he adds that there were new elections to the command posts of the union during the last days of the conflict. The dissatisfaction was great among the workers, who "figured that they had lost the strike", and many of them abandoned the union.

A man who had closely followed the strike, Bernard Shane of the International Ladies' Garment Workers' Union, later tried to revive the militancy of the working girls.

Born in New Jersey, Bernard Shane had devoted the largest part of his adult life to the organization of workers within the International Ladies' Garment Workers' Union (ILGWU). His first visit to Canada brought him to Toronto in 1929, to unionize the workers of the coat-making industry. He succeeded, directed a one-week strike which was crowned with a victory, and kept the union operating for two years. Afterwards, he went to Chicago, where he was again active among the garment workers.

In 1934 the international president of the ILGWU, David Dubinsky (who one year later, with John L. Lewis, was a founder of the Committee for Industrial Organization), asked Bernard Shane to go to Montréal. The coat workers in Toronto had succeeded in rousing their union, which had temporarily fallen into apathy after the departure of Shane, and they had just signed a new contract with the employers.

But the market of the Montréal and Toronto firms was essentially the same, and the Toronto workers feared that they would lose out to competition from the non-unionized shops in Montréal.

Dubinsky therefore asked Shane to go to Montréal to see what could be done. "You will probably only stay there three weeks," the international president had told his organizer. "I don't believe that you can do much there." He expected that the combined forces of clerical anti-unionism and of the anti-international unionism of the needle trades workers would block any efforts by the ILGWU in Montréal.

Shane arrived in Montréal on a cold day in February 1934. Forty years later he was still there.

His first efforts were directed at the coat industry workers. He went to a regional meeting of workers and submitted his plans to them. He was immediately attacked by radical elements who accused him of coming to Montréal only to spoil the season to the profit of Toronto, of being an agent of the Toronto employers.

Refusing to be discouraged, he told himself that the best means of penetrating the coat-making industry was to obtain the cooperation of a group of craftsmen indispensible to its operation. He first addressed himself to the pressers, proposing that they go on strike and assuring them that if they did they would get a raise of $5 over the $18 a week which they were getting. But the pressers, like the radicals, accused him of seeking only to ruin the season.

He then directed his campaign at the cutters, and there he had more success. The cutters let themselves be convinced, went on strike in March, and obtained from ten firms a minimum salary of $30 for a 44-hour week, compared to the $18 which they previously earned for a week with no limit on the number of hours.

After the victory of the cutters, the non-specialized workers and the other craft workers in the coat sector flocked to the ILGWU. In July, following a strike threat which was never executed, conditions were improved, although not as much as the union demanded.

The union had called for a 20 per cent raise and the 40-hour week. It obtained a 40 per cent raise for the cutters who prepared the autumn fashions (they constituted about three per cent of the manpower), and a 10 per cent raise for the least paid workers, but most of the salaries stayed essentially the same. The employers conceded the 44-hour week and promised not to require overtime except in the weeks just preceding the seasonal changes. Even then, no worker would be obliged to do more than six hours of overtime a week. Finally, the employers recognized the union as the legitimate representative of their employees.

This was not a brilliant victory, but the results compared favourably to those which the rival union of Needle Workers obtained two months later in the dressmaking sector.

After the fiasco of the dressmakers' strike, the workers, especially the women, were hesitant to join any union.

But Bernard Shane had resolved to bring all the garment workers in Montréal into the lap of the ILGWU, and he would not hear of abandoning the task so soon after having undertaken it.

Union events at the continental level helped him. In November 1935 the international president of the ILGWU, David Dubinsky, participated with some other American unionists in the formation of a Committee for Industrial Organization which later gave birth to the CIO, a rallying point of worker militancy in North America for a decade. At about the same time the leaders of the Communist movement in Canada ordered the dissolution of the Workers' Unity League and most of the union organizers affiliated to the WUL joined the growing ranks of the CIO. Thus, the CIO started to be synonymous with labour struggle in the industrial centres of the United States and Canada, and the former leaders of the Needle Workers' Industrial Union, in Montréal as in Toronto, Winnipeg and Hamilton, joined in the efforts of the ILGWU, their recent adversary. Not that the fusion took place without conflicts, but at least there were no longer two organizations fighting over the loyalty of the workers.

Against this backdrop Bernard Shane, assisted by the local leaders of the ILGWU in the coat-making sector and those of the Trades and Labour Council of Montréal, pursued his campaign among the workers of the dress industry.

Faithful to his belief that he first had to get specialized craft workers to affiliate, he concentrated in the beginning on cutters in the dress sector. These were, after all, the workers most favourably disposed to unionism. They had had their own independent union before linking their destiny to that of the Needle Workers, and they believed in the protection that collective action offered.

In fact a group of dissident cutters within the Industrial Union had asked for and obtained a charter from the ILGWU even before the strike of 1934 in the dress sector had ended.

However, almost two years went by before the dress cutters came out in the open under their new banner. In April 1936 the ILGWU local which represented them demanded a meeting with the leaders of the management association, the Dress Manufacturers' Guild. This was refused, and some 300 cutters went on strike. After ten days they concluded on agreement with the employers which gave them the 44-hour week at a minimum salary of $30 for cutters and $22 for assistants. In the words of Bernard Shane, the ILGWU had "a foot in the door" in the dress industry.

There was at that time more than one pessimist ready to predict that the ILGWU would never go far, and that it would never win over the French-Canadian working women who now made up almost all of the labour force. The bosses had, to all intents and purposes, purged this sector of the Jewish working women suspected of having been responsible for the strike of 1934.

But the international president David Dubinsky, who had expected so little in 1934, now had faith in the organizing talents of his representative in Montréal. To help him, in September 1936, he sent him a very talented organizer, Rose Pesotta, who had been nourished on libertarian doctrines in her youth and was impassioned with the union cause. Starting from September 10 she obtained a bilingual local radio program, in which several guests from the international unions participated. Assisted by militants from the coat sector, she prepared leaflets, and went door to door to sell the union message to the working girls.

In January 1937 the dressmakers' local received its charter from the international. Unknown to those present, a photographer from the newspaper *L'Illustration Nouvelle* took a picture of the first leaders and published it in his paper the next day. The same day, several who had been photographed were either fired or laid off for an indefinite period. Others suffered the same fate in the following days.

In the wake of these events, the ILGWU decided to declare a strike in the shop where there had been the greatest number of firings. The strikers asked only for the rehiring, without discrimination, of the fired workers. The working girls set up picket lines at the doors to the shop despite the freezing weather typical of a Montréal January. At the end of three days they won their case; a verbal agreement sanctioned their right to join the union of their choice.

The bosses were quite aware that a broader struggle had to come soon. Did the leaders of the Manufacturers' Guild take the first steps, as the "hagiographers" of the ILGWU claim, or did the Canadian and Catholic Confederation of Labour itself take the initiative? This is not yet clearly established. What is known is that the bosses, at the beginning of 1937, concluded an agreement with the Catholic League of Needle Industry Workers, affiliated to the National Clothing Federation within that organization. A hundred employers recognized the Catholic unions as legitimate representatives of their employees.

At the beginning of April 1937, a spokesman for the employers, H.H. Stein, declared that the agreement between bosses and Catholic unions provided for a general salary raise of 15 to 20 per cent, a minimum salary of between $8 and $14 for a 44-hour week for non-specialized workers (excluding the cutters and pressers).

Philippe Girard, an organizer in the progressive wing of the Catholic union who actively participated in the most famous strikes of its affiliates in the late Thirties, maintains that the incursion of the Catholic unions into the needle trades was not purely a tactic of appeasement by the bosses aimed at cutting the ground out from under a more militant and non-religious union. He says that the Catholic unions were simply seeking to assure the protection of thousands of working women neglected by the ILGWU, which was preoccupied with the problems of the craftsmen.

The ILGWU leaders went so far as to charge that the bosses were financing the Catholic unions, and that the Catholic unions were obtaining adherents by threatening the working women with excommunication if they refused to join and turned instead to an international and neutral union.

To reach the French-Canadian women workers, the ILGWU in March 1937 hired young Claude Jodoin as an organizer; he was at that time president of the Young Liberals and later, in 1956, became the first president of the largest Canadian central union organization, the Canadian Labour Congress, where he remained until 1968.

Another French Canadian, Raoul Trépanier, president of the Montréal Trades and Labour Council, was at the top level of the ILGWU recruiting campaign, and when the general strike began in mid-April of 1937, he became the president of the strike committee.

The Montréal local could also count on the unconditional support of the international leadership of the ILGWU. Around the same period, the union had signed several contracts with American employers, and, lo and behold, some of these employers had just installed themselves in Montréal, where they could pay workers much less than the union rates established in the United States. Other employers from across the border were putting pressure on the international, urging it to do something to put an end to the competition from the non-union shops in Montréal.

With this support, and with the example of a strike movement which was then sweeping many urban centres of North America (including Oshawa, Ontario, where the auto workers were occupying their factories), the working men and women of the Montréal dress industry, after futile attempts to start negotiations with the management association, began a general strike on the morning of April 15, 1937.

In order not to alert the bosses, the starting time of the strike was not announced. On the night of the 14th and 15th, militants visited the workers in their homes to inform them and to invite them not to go to work the next day.

At dawn on the 15th, certain militants visited the shops and, following the tactics already used in strikes in this industry, shut off the power and stopped the machines.

Others harangued the working men and women as they arrived at work. Rapidly the great majority of some 4,000 workers in the dress sector rallied to the strike action. The garment district, from Peel Street to Bleury Street, and the length of St. Catherine, was back on slack time.

The newspapers marked this strike as being the first thrust of the Congress of Industrial Organizations in Québec. The union distributed financial aid (of $4 to $7 per week), opened a free canteen, paid medical bills and other urgent needs of the strikers.

During the first days there were some arrests of union members who were participating on picket lines. The union leaders had to deal rigourously with those of their followers who wanted to play poker or pinochle to fill the long hours of idleness: playing cards for money on union premises would have furnished the city police with too good a pretext for raiding.

From the beginning of the conflict there was evidence of a split within the management association. Some of its members threatened to dissociate themselves from the others, to form their own group and to open talks with the union. The spring and summer dress season was just beginning. Certain employers foresaw that a prolonged strike could bring them to bankruptcy.

But the president of the Dress Manufacturers' Guild, Charles Sommer, sounded the alarm. This strike was the first incursion of the CIO on the local scene, he declared, and the bosses had to fight it stubbornly.

Certain elements of the clergy shared the views of Mr. Sommer. On Sunday, May 18, in the pulpits of Montréal churches, a letter was read from the chaplain general of the Catholic unions, Jean Bertrand of the Sulpicians. This letter was also signed by two other priests from the same order, Conrad Block and Jean-Baptiste Desrosiers.

In substance, the letter said that with the approval of Cardinal Villeneuve of Québec, the reverend abbés urged the workers not to join the international union; it demanded that the government arrest and deport "foreign agents" and "Communists" who were leading the ILGWU.

"Poor Bernard Shane," a militant of the period later commented, "was accused of being a Communist, he who saw them under every bed."

On Monday the 19th, the secretary general of the Canadian and Catholic Confederation of Labour, Gérard Picard, signed an article published in the Québec daily, *L'Action Catholique,* attacking the legitimacy of the ILGWU. As the latter had not obtained incorporation from the government under the professional unions law, a procedure that the Catholic unions were almost alone in following in that period, Mr. Picard concluded that it was outside the law.

For his part, the general president of the Catholic union, Alfred Charpentier, told the strikers to return to work and called on the municipal police chief, Fernand Dufresne, for special protection for those who would follow his advice.

In the Québec legislature, Premier Maurice Duplessis was still in the first hours of a regime which would turn out to be a long one. His Minister of Labour, William Tremblay, charged one of his civil servants, Clovis Bernier, to offer his services to the two parties as a mediator and arbitrator.

Already the representatives of the ILGWU were holding meetings with the dissident group of employers from the Dress Manufacturers' Guild who formed their own "Dress Manufacturers' Organization".

The union demanded a general salary raise of 20 per cent, with a minimum of $12.50 for the non-specialized workers and of $30 for the cutters, the 44-hour week, time-and-a-half for overtime, and the recognition of the ILGWU.

About a week after the start of the strike, 40 to 50 manufacturers dissented from the official association, the Guild, and concluded agreements with the ILGWU. The salary raises agreed to were 10 per cent, instead of the 20 per cent demanded by the workers at the beginning, but the employers involved agreed to meet with the union as the legitimate representative of their employees.

The president of the Guild, Mr. Sommer, declared that the firms which had concluded agreements were insignificant in the industry and only affected about five per cent of the total production. He reiterated the firm resolution of the majority of the employers to combat "the intrusion of the CIO" to the end.

"If this so-called labour organization succeeds in forcing the manufacturers to recognize it," he said to the *Montreal Daily Star,* "in a short time it will penetrate into other industries. Then the troubles will accumulate until the CIO dominates Canadian manpower and each Canadian worker becomes the vassal of the tsars of American unionism. We are well decided to combat this attempt to force Canadian workers to enter the ranks of an organization which in the United States is a law unto itself. The Canadian workers respect the law and they respect their contracts. We refuse to negotiate with any organization which breaks its contracts and destroys the industry."

Despite the fears of the manufacturers, the strike remained peaceable enough, and was marked by very few arrests. On April 20, of the four accused who appeared before the court in cases related to the conflict, only two were union members; the other two were former provincial policemen accused of assault against the strikers. All were jailed while awaiting trial.

On Saturday, April 24, the provincial deputy minister of labour, Gérard Tremblay, called a meeting of the representatives of the employers, the ILGWU and the Catholic unions. Mr. Sommer, on behalf of the employers, agreed to grant a raise of 10 per cent (rather than 20) to the strikers, as well as the 44-hour week with time-and-a-half for overtime after 48 hours, all on condition that the employees return to work the following Monday and that the other disputed questions, as the deputy minister suggested, be submitted to arbitration.

According to the newspaper reports, the union leaders had accepted the offer on condition that the strikers accept it in their turn. There would be many debates in the following days concerning this presumed agreement.

But previously, in the presence of the deputy-minister, a quarrel had broken out between the spokesmen of the ILGWU and that of the Catholic unions, Alfred Charpentier, general president of the CCCL.

Mr. Charpentier denied the accusations of the ILGWU that the Catholic unions were in the pay of the employer. One of the ILGWU lawyers, Louis Fitch, retorted: "I have no doubt at all that the Catholic League is made up of good people. I see that there is a priest here today among their representatives, and if these were not good people, I am sure that Father Bertrand would not mix with them. We are only complaining about the fact that the manufacturers have exploited their goodness."

For his part, the president of the Guild, Mr. Sommer, made a surprising declaration at the same meeting. He asserted that the employers had always been disposed to negotiate with their employees. He had been very surprised, on arriving at his firm the morning of the strike, to discover that the cutters were on strike. The conditions of the cutters, he noted, were already settled by a contract which would not finish until January 1938, and there could be no question, whatever might happen, of consenting to give them another salary increase before this date.

The strike entered its second week, and despite the hopes entertained following the Saturday meeting, the workers did not seem to have any intention of returning to work. In Québec the minister of labour, William Tremblay, was becoming nervous. On Wednesday he sent the following message to the president of the strike committee and of the Montréal Trades and Labour Council, Raoul Trépanier:

"Following the offer to arbitrate the conflict in the dress industry made by the Ministry of Labour, you are by these presents advised by the government of this province that the manufacturers have accepted the said offer and that the union has not yet given its answer after three days of requested delay. I urge you to accept arbitration within 24 hours and to have the employees return to work. Your attitude does wrong to all the firms linked to the garment industry, without speaking of the damages inflicted on the dress industry, and causes unemployment throughout the province. A refusal on your part to comply with the conditions mentioned above would authorize the ministry to seriously examine any act of conspiracy aiming at creating intolerable disorders. Your demand for the closed union shop cannot be considered as an acceptable justification for new delays. Please respond by telegram today."

Bernard Shane, leader of the ILGWU, immediately denied having promised the deputy minister to have the strikers return by Monday the 26th. "I never told him that and even if I had said it," he declared to the newspapers, "I strongly doubt that the strikers would have agreed to go back."

As for Raoul Trépanier, he responded to the minister by telegram:

"Had formal agreement with deputy minister that we not give our answer before Wednesday evening. Deny that we were harming garment-related industries. Alleged arguments for or by the associated industries inspired by the Guild. Declaration about unemployment throughout province equally fictitious and unfounded. Suggestion we create intolerable disorders offensive and we deny it. No disorders have happened in strike and will happen only if employers persist in using agents provocateurs. Have to now and will continue to lead present strike peaceably and legitimately whatever others do. As president of the Montréal Trades and Labour Council representing 50,000 workers and president of Québec bureau of the Trades and Labour Congress of Canada representing 127,000 workers across country am shocked and stupefied at tone of your telegram suggesting that peaceable and legitimate strike affecting thousands of dissatisfied workers be considered act of conspiracy."

The next day the Minister affirmed that he had not issued an ultimatum to the strikers but had simply warned them that if they did not return to work in 24 hours new difficulties would arise for them.

On Friday, Premier Maurice Duplessis entered the fray. He declared to the parliamentary journalists that as attorney general he would order the arrest and detention without bail of Bernard Shane and Raoul Trépanier on charges of conspiracy against the public order, and declared that he would not tolerate any Communist infiltration. He had recently had the "padlock law" adopted, allowing him to close down any premises used for Communist purposes or where Communist writings were found. The law did not define the meaning of the word "communist". Much later this law was ruled unconstitutional by the Supreme Court of Canada.

Meanwhile, by Saturday morning, May 1, no arrest had yet been made. The ILGWU lawyer, Mr. Fitch, declared to the press that Messrs. Trépanier and Shane had heard nothing about the arrest warrants issued against them except what they had read in the newspapers.

Mr. Fitch added that without a doubt the Premier had been misquoted, that he could not have declared that all bail would be refused to the strikers' leaders, since such a decision belonged to the judges. "He doubtless meant to say," added the lawyer, "that the provincial police have received an order to detain the accused without provisional release until they appear in Court, a more and more current practice in Québec."

Raoul Trépanier declared that he was at the disposal of the Premier or of his emissaries, who could find him at his office. "Mr. Duplessis has the power to have me arrested, although I doubt that he has the right," he said.

The union leaders feared that the police would delay the time of arrest until the courts adjourned for the week-end, thus forcing the accused to spend two days in the infamous cells of the provincial police headquarters.

Candide Rochefort, provincial deputy for Ste. Marie, a Montréal riding with a strong concentration of workers, returned to Montréal from Québec to ensure the uninterrupted leadership of the strike if the two leaders were arrested.

Mr. Rochefort declared to the press: "We will never accept a contract which will be unilateral. We will not capitulate and the Premier is very badly informed about the strike. There is a trust in the dress industry and I would recommend to Mr. Duplessis to follow the example of the plan of President Roosevelt (of the United States), who wants the workers to obtain the best possible conditions from their employers. If each person in the province of Québec who seeks to improve his salary and his working conditions has to be treated like a Communist, one will see that the Communists will be very numerous. Premier Duplessis endangers the liberty of individuals who demand better living conditions."

During the weekend there were talks with the authorities, the nature and the content of which still remain confidential more than thirty years later. In any case, neither Mr. Shane nor Mr. Trépanier was arrested.

On Monday, in Québec, the Legislative Assembly of the province dedicated almost the entire day to debating the Montréal dress strike and the order for the arrest of Trépanier and Shane issued by the Premier. The latter had to receive the criticisms of certain members of his own party, the Union Nationale, formed the preceding year. The debate centered around the examination of the budget of the Ministry of Labour and was mainly a procedural duel between the spokesmen of the Liberal opposition and the government leaders on the possibility of discussing a strike during the examination of a budget.

Premier Duplessis nevertheless took the opportunity to express his viewpoint on unionism and strikes, a viewpoint which he would maintain without much change until his death twenty-two years later.

"Although the government is ready and desirous to protect the interests of the working class of this province," he said, "the government will not permit union leaders to infringe the law in the pursuit of their demands."

He declared that despite all the efforts of authentically Québécois union leaders, the Communists had succeeded in imposing their ideas on certain unions, and that the government intended to take all necessary measures to stop the progress of such practices and ideas.

Mr. Duplessis praised his colleague, Ontario Premier Mitchell Hepburn, who very recently, during the occupation of factories by the auto workers in Oshawa, had fired his Minister of Labour for being too soft, taken over the portfolio himself, and warned the CIO organizers that the worst awaited them if they persisted in their campaign among the Ontario workers.

Mr. Hepburn, according to Mr. Duplessis, had shown "firmness and courage against the American labour agitators" and le Chef — as this Québec premier was afterwards called—deplored that the Canadian government had not adopted the same attitude in forbidding these agitators access to the country.

Despite this support given to the bosses by the highest public authority in the province, the conflict would be settled that same week. On Tuesday Issachar Greenberg, who was in that period the arbitrator of conflicts in the coat industry, proposed to the belligerents that they participate in a meeting at his office.

On Thursday, May 6, at two o'clock in the morning, after a marathon of uninterrupted negotiations which had gone on since noon of the previous day, the ILGWU representatives left Mr. Greenberg's office with an agreement in their pocket. The following Monday, May 10, the strikers returned to work. The conflict had lasted a little more than three weeks.

The agreement provided for a general salary increase of 10 per cent, the 44-hour five-and-a-half-day week with time-and-a-half for overtime, a procedure for hearing and settling the grievances of the workers, the right to set rates for piece work, and—despite the recent management irredentism on this subject—a total recognition of the union, whose members alone could work in the establishments signatory to the agreement.

The contract also said that the minimal salary scales would have to be fixed by an impartial arbitrator. At the end of May, an arbitrator was named and after long discussions he established norms which, in the opinion of the union, were equivalent to a revolution in the industry. For a large number of working girls the arbitration meant a raise of $4 to $5 a week. Certain of them who were previously paid $11 for an 80-hour week now received $16 for a 44-hour week.

The exultation of the workers when they returned to work was of short duration. The accounts of eye-witnesses agree on one point: the contract, once signed, was very poorly observed. It is on the causes of this semi-failure that the interpretations vary.

Bernard Shane, in a document dating from 1962, affirms that the blame should be placed on the Communist elements, former leaders of the Needle Workers' Industrial Union, within the ILGWU local.

"Time passed and the internal struggle that the Communists were waging within the union began to take effect," he said. "We were a young workers' organization, most of whose members had never joined a union before. When this internal battle began, several lost confidence and drew away.

"The bosses, who had not folded their tents in the face of the Union, profited from this weakness. Little by little they neglected to respect the clauses of the labour contract. The more they ignored the requirements of the contract, the more the workers were apathetic."

Other people, other interpretations. Some stress what they see as the real progress brought about by the strike. Friday afternoons at five o'clock for example —because overtime was not allowed on Friday—all the workers and all the working girls left the shops together, at five o'clock, while it was still daylight: this was a "revolution".

And the union shop, also, changed a lot of things. Essentially it meant the death of management favouritism. If the boss needed an employee, whether a cutter or a finisher, he had to address himself to the union. And the union referred him to the person who had been longest unemployed.

But the union shop, in certain cases, had to lead to a new form of favouritism, this time in the union. In some establishments the bosses used their ingenuity to cajole the union delegates, and sometimes they succeeded, through favours and gifts.

If the union delegate was inclined to the management side, the ordinary members could do little. The workers had never had a written copy of the contract which had been signed in their name. They were forced to rely on the word of their delegates.

Militants tried to complain in the union meetings about the compromises of certain delegates, but the union leadership accused all its critics of being Communists. In the shops many workers lost confidence in any union organization whatsoever. Bernard Shane says that around 1939 the ILGWU only had the support of about a third of the workers in the dress industry.

So when a new strike broke out in the dress industry on April 22, 1940, its aim was not only to obtain better conditions, but also to breathe new life into a union which seemed to be on the path to extinction, and to prove to the bosses that the ILGWU could still count on the loyalty of the working girls.

The strikers demanded a general raise of 10 per cent. Negotiations got underway almost as soon as the conflict began, and the Manufacturers' Guild offered a five per

cent immediate increase, with another five per cent starting in September 1940.

The ILGWU leaders knew that the strikers would
resist this compromise, so they invited the Mayor of
Montréal, Camilien Houde, to their meeting. He urged
the working girls to accept the compromise proposed by
their union leaders, and the working men and women of
the dress industry followed the advice of their mayor.
On April 30 they went back on the job.

But the ILGWU still had the task of creating
unity in its ranks. During an internal debate on an increase in union dues from 25 to 35 cents a week, a group
of radicals, some of them Communists, were accused of
sabotaging union action. After trial by the union, several
were expelled from the ILGWU. Since the employers
had conceded the union shop, and since one had to be
a member of the union to get work, these sanctions
meant that the dissidents could no longer find a job in
the dress industry in Montréal.

From 1940 to 1970 there were no more strikes by
working girls in the garment industry in Montréal.

chapter four

the "bleuets" strikes

Around Lac Saint-Jean, which seems as big as a sea, and along the banks of the Saguenay, more majestic than many rivers, lies a region whose inhabitants have been so successful in developing their own history, customs and manner of speaking that they have created a sort of province within Québec. These settlers are called "Bleuets", from the name of the little blue berry, cousin of the myrtle, which abounds in the thickets of the region.

The economy of Lac Saint-Jean has two sources of nourishment: aluminum and the forest industry, and in each of them, during the Second World War, spectacular labour conflicts unfolded and directly influenced government policies.

The first of these strikes was already over when it captured the attention of Canadian and Québec public opinion on July 29, 1941. On that day the federal Minister of Supply, C.D. Howe, father of modern technocracy in Canada, announced during a press conference that the Alcan (Aluminum Company of Canada) factory in Arvida had been seized by a few men and that 9,000 others were idle as a result. He explained that sabotage was suspected; that Alcan, supplier of aluminum for airplane construction, was the most important war industry in the country; and that the strike which had taken place there had been the most important interruption of war production in Canada since the outbreak of the world conflict.

The Minister added that two companies of soldiers —400 military personnel in all—had been sent onto the premises, and that it could take three weeks to put the big vats "frozen" during the walkout back into operation. The strike, said Howe, had affected 5,000 Alcan workers plus 4,000 construction workers who had gone out on a sympathy strike in support of the action by the Alcan employees.

The details of the conflict would not be known outside of the Lac Saint-Jean region until several months later, in mid-October, when the Royal Commission charged with investigating the events, made up of two judges of the Court of King's Bench, submitted its report.

However, well before that report, C.D. Howe had the government adopt an Order-in-Council facilitating the mobilization of troops in case of social unrest. He had found that in Arvida it had taken too long to get all the authorization necessary before the army could intervene.

The investigating commissioners, Judges Séverin Létourneau and W.L. Bond, discovered a whole package of causes leading to the work stoppage at Alcan on July 24, 1941.

First of all, the company had dragged its feet in responding to salary demands which the workers had presented on many occasions. The recent demand had been presented in May, and there had still been no response by July.

The salaries of the vat workers had been fixed in 1940 at $125 to $130 per month, but there were amounts held back, such as payments to a pension fund and donations to the Catholic Church. There was a bonus tied to the rate of production, but its amount varied from month to month.

The salaries paid to the aluminum workers on July 24 were lower than usual: there were accumulated deductions for the national defence tax and for the new unemployment insurance system. The production bonus was reduced, and the cost-of-living indemnity normally paid in wartime was missing from the pay envelope.

In addition, there was a heat wave in late July of 1941. The mercury climbed to 90 degrees Fahrenheit on the 23rd, then to 94.5 degrees on the 24th outside the factory, and it is said that in the vat rooms the temperature went up to 125 degrees. The heat slowed down the pace of production and workers feared that their pay, which was tied to the production level, would also be lower.

The oily rags only needed a spark to set them on fire. On July 23 a man was missing from the team responsible for operating vats 40 and 41. The team from vats 42 and 42a had to take up the slack, each man having to take care of nine or ten vats. At suppertime the men of the team on 40 and 41 accused those of the team on 42 and 42a of being soft on the company in agreeing to relieve absent workers. Nothing more was needed. The argument which followed led to the decision to go on strike.

At four o'clock on the 24th the strike began. The danger to the vats was only realized two hours later. The aluminum was melted down in these giant boilers, and they had to be heated constantly; otherwise they would suffer considerable damage. The danger was remembered too late — the vats were already "frozen". It was later established by the Royal Commission that war production of aluminum was reduced by 32,000,000 pounds, at a cost to the company of more than six million dollars.

The union, affiliated to the Canadian and Catholic Confederation of Labour, had called a meeting before the walkout for the evening of July 24. The union was planning to demand the formation of a conciliation board to settle the dispute between the company and its employees. But when the time for the meeting came the workers were already on strike.

On July 24 the strike covered the whole factory. Only the heating and electrical systems continued to function. The general manager of the factory, Mr. A.C. Johnson, read a declaration to the strikers describing their strike as illegal. But the Town of Arvida only had five policemen and the majority, if not all, of the 33 company security guards took the side of the strikers. Worried, the general manager appealed to the federal Minister of Labour, who sent a conciliator, Mr. M.S. Campbell. The Québec government also delegated a conciliator, Mr. Cyprien Miron.

The federal conciliator, Mr. Campbell, who was unilingually English, learned from witnesses that the Catholic union had not encouraged the strike movement, which had been started outside of the union hierarchy. Mr. Campbell misunderstood, and believed that instead of the strike being blamed on elements "outside the union", it was being blamed on "outside agitators". From this came the thesis, later amplified by the Minister, C.D. Howe, that sabotage linked to the enemies of the country was involved. The investigating commissioners later would refuse to recognize the validity of this thesis, and would even go so far as to strongly deny it.

But meanwhile, the interpretation of Mr. Campbell had gone to Ottawa, where the government decided to have troops intervene. On the 27th two companies arrived from the Valcartier military base, near Québec City, accompanied by a detachment of provincial police.

Already, a few thousand construction workers, employed by the Foundation Company for the expansion of the Alcan plant, had joined the aluminum workers. Hundreds of workers were occupying the factory, and would continue to do so until the police evicted them on July 28.

The company then offered to bring the salary of the vat workers up to 51 cents an hour, to pay the cost-of-living indemnity, and to submit the entire dispute to a conciliation board.

On July 28 the strikers pronounced themselves against returning to work by a vote of 2,452 to 50. It was then that the Secretary General of the Canadian and Catholic Conferation of Labour, Mr. Gérard Picard, intervened.

On July 29, facing the strikers massed on the Arvida golf course, Mr. Picard appealed to reason. The strikers listened to him; at a quarter to four in the afternoon the president of the union, Alexis Daris, announced to the company that the workers agreed to go back, and at four o'clock, work resumed. The strike had lasted five days, but its echo had been heard from the east to the west coast of Canada.

From August 1 the salary of the vat workers was raised to 51 cents an hour, benefiting some 900 workers who previously had received only 49 cents an hour. In addition, all the workers received the cost-of-living indemnity of $1.25 a week.

The accusations of sabotage were rejected by the Royal Commission of Inquiry. The Commission found that the company had shown negligence in its relations with the workers, and particularly reproached it for not having posted the government notice explaining the illegality of strikes under certain circumstances. The investigators concluded that the local management had perhaps suffered from the constraints imposed on it by the head office in Montréal.

The CCCL, weak up to then, took on a new boldness after this conflict. It hired its first permanent organizer, a young graduate of the no less young School of Social Sciences of Laval University, Jean Marchand. The union had him establish himself in Lac Saint-Jean. His arrival is generally given as a cause of the awakening which led to a series of strikes in the pulp and paper factories of the region. These strikes provoked the creation of another Royal Commission of Inquiry, presided over by Judge J. A. Prévost of the Court of King's Bench, and including Judges Stuart McDougall of the same Court and Garon Pratte of the Superior Court. Their report served as the basis for the working out of labour legislation whose principles, after more than a quarter of a century, still guide labour relations in Québec.

The Catholic union had won members in the pulp and paper industry of Lac Saint-Jean around the middle Thirties. But the companies refused to negotiate with them. The international unions arrived later—the Brotherhood of Paper Workers, and the Brotherhood of Pulp, Sulfite and Paper Mill Workers, both affiliated to the

American Federation of Labour and the Canadian Trades and Labour Congress.

The companies agreed to deal with the international unions. There are several explanations for this. First of all, the "internationals" recruited paper-makers, highly-specialized workers who were few in number in each factory but indispensible to their operation. Then—and the employers later related this argument to the Prévost Commission—the international unions made it clear to management that if it did not deal with them, other unions affiliated with the American Federation of Labour, both in the paper industry and in the printing industry, would refuse, even in the United States, to let their members use products not made by members of the same organization. Since the pulp and paper market was above all an export market, the argument was a cutting one. Finally—and it is Professor Jean-Réal Cardin, in his pamphlet entitled "L'influence du syndicalisme national catholique sur le droit syndical québécois", who offers this hypothesis—it is believed that the employers, Anglophones for the most part, preferred to deal with unions whose leaders were also Anglophones and of a similar mentality, rather than with a Catholic and Francophone group.

In 1940, in factories in the Lac Saint-Jean district and elsewhere, the companies conceded contract clauses to the international unions anticipating the closed union shop: the employees retained their freedom with regards to union bodies, but all the new employees were bound to join the internationals.

Tension mounted as a result of this clause. In March 1943 the gunpowder caught fire. In the mills of the Price Brothers Company in Jonquière, Kénogami and Riverbend, a comfortable majority of the workers signed a petition informing the company that they did not want to be represented by the international unions but instead chose the Catholic union affiliated to the Pulp and Paper Federation. The Company did not respond, and on April 5 the Catholic unions of the three factories asked the Canadian Department of Labour to form a conciliation board to study their case. Because of faulty drafting this request could not be agreed to immediately. Meanwhile the company advised fourteen employees that they would be fired at once if they did not pay the dues they owed to the international unions. This was the immediate cause of the strike, which began on April 6 at the Riverbend factory and spread the next day to the Jonquière and Kénogami factories.

The strike lasted 10 days. It ended on April 16, thanks to the intervention of the Québec Ministry of Labour, which obtained a promise from the company that the contract between it and the international unions expiring on May 15 would not be renewed until a conciliation board had ruled on the inter-union conflict.

If this agreement temporarily satisfied the members of the Catholic unions, it provoked the wrath of the international unions. The paper-makers in their turn stopped work to protest against what appeared to them to be a breach of contract. A new accord, concluded on April 23, restored peace: it provided for the creation of a royal commission of inquiry and the upholding of existing contracts until the presentation of the report of this commission, except that the closed union shop clause would be suspended starting on May 15.

But before the presentation of the report another conflict, similar to the first ones, broke out in the mills of the Lake St. John Power and Paper Company at Dolbeau. There the company had renewed its contracts with the international unions in May 1943, despite the protests of members of the Catholic unions. Moreover, at the beginning of June it had hired a worker from outside the region as a paper-maker, while the union claimed that there were already several competent candidates. Around the same period the company advised eighteen workers that they would be suspended if they did not pay their dues to the international unions. The strike broke out on June 6, 1943, while the Prévost Commission was holding its public hearings. The strike ended on July 1, after the Québec Minister of Labour had promised the workers that their case would also be submitted to the

Commission. The settlement resembled the one which had put an end to the April conflict, except that the closed shop clause was maintained. The workers who did not settle with the international unions obtained permission to deposit what they owed with the clerk of the Prévost Commission until the Commission submitted its report.

In its report, transmitted to the Lieutenant-Governor on August 25, 1943, the Commission, with the clarity of the best jurists and in highly elegant language, proposed the adoption of new labour legislation which would guarantee union freedom but would at the same time offer mechanisms under government control capable of establishing which union was the most representative of the workers in a factory. While waiting for general legislation, it recommended the holding of a vote by secret ballot among the pulp and paper workers involved in the dispute, to determine which union should represent them. The result was a victory for the Catholic unions among the production workers, while the international unions maintained their position among the paper-makers.

chapter five

the tramway strikes

The year 1943, the fourth year of the war, was a tumultuous one for Québec workers. In all, 103 labour conflicts were recorded, of which several, involving thousands of workers, were spectacular. But the most unusual strikes of all were without a doubt those that hit the Montréal public services that year: first mass transit, then the city's manual employees, who went back on strike a few months later to support the strike of the police and firefighters, and finally the city's office workers, whose conflict continued until the beginning of the following year.

The transport conflict in some respects set the tone for the others. In that era public transport was handled mainly by tramways — what Montréalers called "petits chars", or steetcars — with buses only providing a small part of the service. The service was supplied by a private company, Montreal Tramways, whose business was then going well: in 1942 it had transported 319,398,324 people, an increase of 55,826,536 over 1941. The geographic expansion of the city and the resurgence of business brought about by the war explain this upswing.

One can imagine the prosperity enjoyed by the company when one knows that for the year 1943 the profit-sharing bonuses granted to some 3,800 employees varied between $400 and $650 each. These bonuses were a redistribution of one quarter of the company's revenues, which exceeded fifteen million dollars.

It was just these bonuses which were at the origin of the conflict that thrice paralyzed mass transit in Montréal between March 1943 and August 1944.

At Montreal Tramways there had been two unions for twenty years. All this was going on before Canadian and Québec labour legislation decreed that there could only be one union to a company. One, a section of the Amalgamated Street and Electrical Railway and Motor Coach Employees of America, known as Local 790 and affiliated with the American Federation of Labour, signed the contracts with the employer. The second, the Tramways' Employees' Union, affiliated to the Canadian and Catholic Confederation of Labour and known simply as the 'Catholic Union', did not sign the contract but could count on the adherence of about 800 workers and had the right to submit grievances to management. In 1940 a third union entered the picture, the Canadian Brotherhood of Railroad, Transport and General Workers, affiliated with the Canadian Congress of Labour which itself was associated with the Congress of Industrial Organizations. Its arrival marked a turning point in the life of mass transit employees in Montréal.

It all began in July 1940, when Local 790 signed a contract with Montreal Tramways for a duration of three years or until the end of the war, if it lasted longer. Article 110 of the contract read as follows:

"The gross receipts of the company deriving from tramways and bus passengers (but excluding the receipts deriving from rented tramways and buses), for the period of twelve (12) consecutive months ending on June 30 of each year during the period of this contract, will be compiled by the company in less than ten (10) days after the end of each period. If the gross receipts of one of these periods exceeds the figure of fifteen (15) million, the Company will deduct 25% of the excess to constitute a fund which will be applied to the supplementary remuneration of those of the employees who are not superior agents and who:

a) have earned $2,500 or less and who

b) have been continually on the payrolls of the Company during the period in question.

Each of these employees will receive a share of this fund, which will be the same percentage of this fund as the percentage of his salary with regard to the total salary of the employees qualified to benefit from the fund for the said period. The Company will pay its employees their respective shares before the 31st of the month of July which follows the end of the period."

All this seemed perfect, but lo and behold, in November 1941, the federal government issued a decree limiting the permissible bonus to employees to $50 a year for the duration of the war.

This order-in-council, bearing the number P.C. 8253, stated in article 16 that: "Any provision of a collective labour agreement which is incompatible with the provisions of the present decree must be modified so as to make it conform to the present decree by January 1, 1942 at the latest."

On November 26, only a few days after the promulgation of the decree, Montreal Tramways sent the Québec regional committee of the National Wartime Labour Council a letter declaring that article 110 of the contract which it had signed two years earlier with its employees was abrogated because of the Order-in-Council. To replace it, it offered to pay its employees a weekly cost-of-living bonus of $1.15.

On June 2, 1942, the Québec Regional Committee handed down its decision: the cost-of-living bonus for the tramways employees would have to be $1.80 per week. Only the Brotherhood used the legislative provisions permitting an appeal to contest the decision at that time. The Committee had concluded that this cost-of-living bonus replaced the profit-sharing bonus provided for in the collective agreement, and maintained its decision.

This perhaps could have been a lesser evil, if the rest of the working conditions of the mass transit employees had been advantageous. But such was not the case.

The salaries varied between 36 and 62 cents an hour. For about 10 per cent of the employees directly involved in transportation, like the conductors and drivers, the motormen and machinists, the salary rarely exceeded $10 per week. It also frequently happened that some employees, while having to be on call at least twice a day, did not get work and consequently, did not get paid. There were too many employees for the normal work load.

The employees were not paid for statutory holidays.

They did not get vacation pay, and furthermore the annual vacations which are now the norm did not exist. They did not receive sick pay either, except for what was guaranteed them by their contributions to a mutual assurance fund, — $10 a week in case of illness lasting more than seven days. Employees who had served 25 years with the company could also draw a pension of $50 a month from this fund, made up of dues they had paid, once they reached the age of 60.

Given these conditions, it is not surprising that the tramway employees were extremely angered by the abolition of the profit-sharing bonus. There is no doubt that cost-of-living bonuses were limited by government decree in all firms. But elsewhere, and particularly in the munitions factories and other war industries, the salaries were higher at the beginning and the bonus was only the icing on the cake. Work in public transport could seem to be manna from heaven in the black hours of the Depression, when employment was scarce everywhere. But now, with the industrial upsurge brought on by the war, this was no longer true, if it ever had been.

This was fertile ground for militant unionism. But Local 790, as well as the Catholic union, did not seem able or willing to take advantage of this situation. At the same time, the militant approach of the American union body formed a few years earlier, the Congress of Industrial Organizations, and of its Canadian counterpart, the Canadian Congress of Labour, was also making its mark in Québec.

The general president of the CCL was Aaron Mosher, also president of the Brotherhood of Railwaymen, one of the first industrial unions in Canada of which he had been one of the founders in 1908. At the Brotherhood's convention in 1939 it was decided to recruit systematically among groups other than the railroad employees.

The first local of the Brotherhood among the Montréal Tramway employees was founded in 1940. It grouped the bus drivers, who in that period were only a small minority of the employees in a company that was mainly based on streetcars. The first president was Paul-Émile Marquette, who would soon leave his mark on several industries as a CCL organizer in Québec.

In 1940 the Brotherhood tried to obtain recognition as the representative of the bus drivers in the negotiations for a new contract. Its efforts were in vain.

During the next two years the Brotherhood extended itself little by little to other employees of Montreal Tramways whose allegiance it had not had at first: streetcar employees, and workers in the garages and in the electrical power station. In September 1941 it undertook a campaign to obtain a cost-of-living bonus similar to what other companies were conceding. (This was before the quarrel over the profit-sharing bonus.) This campaign ended in failure.

Finally, at the beginning of 1943, the Brotherhood won over the company's clerks and cashiers. It could henceforth claim to speak in the name of the employees in all sectors of Montreal Tramways. The coordinating committee of the four union sections (buses, tramways, maintenance and offices) demanded of the Company that a vote be held to decide who, the Brotherhood or the two established unions, represented the majority of the employees. This request was rejected and at the beginning of March 1943 the Brotherhood asked the federal government, in conformity with the prevailing legislation, to set up a conciliation board to settle the question of representativity. The Minister of Labour welcomed the request, and on March 16, 1943, he appointed Mr. Bernard Rose of Montréal to preside over the board.

Tension mounted among the employees, as much over the working conditions as over the increasingly sharp inter-union rivalries. On March 26, at the Youville shops where the company manufactured streetcars, a limited strike broke out. Its aim was to protest against the firing of two members of the Brotherhood, Mike Eden and Albert Howard, who were accused of removing a notice from the walls of the shop in which Local 790 attacked the Brotherhood.

The powder caught fire on March 27. The bargaining committee, made up of representatives of Local 790 and the Catholic union, announced that it would hold a referendum with the agreement of the company and on its property, and that the ballot would read as follows:

> "The National Wartime Labour Council has just changed. This change gives the bargaining committee the possibility of making new efforts on salaries. Are you willing to give the bargaining committee all the support it needs to undertake these overtures in your name?"

This question on the ballot required a yes or no answer. A negative response could give the impression that the employee did not want overtures made in his name to increase his salary. An affirmative answer, on the other hand, was equivalent to a vote of confidence in the two established unions. The leaders of the Brotherhood demanded that the company withdraw its agreement to the holding of this vote, which they saw as a trap. The company refused, and the Brotherhood called a general meeting of its members at the Atwater Market for the evening of Sunday, March 28.

The assembly, which brought together some 2,500 of the 3,000 Montreal Tramways employees, was chaired by the president of the Montréal Labour Council (affiliated to the CCL), Mr. Théo Prézeau. Before taking the vote, Paul-Émile Marquette, who had become general director of the union, read to those present a telegram which he had just received from the general president of the Brotherhood, A.R. Mosher. The latter informed the union members of an exchange which he had had the same day with the federal Minister of Labour, Mr. Humphrey Mitchell. The Minister proposed to the members of the Brotherhood that an arbitration tribunal be formed to settle their dispute and made it known to them that if this proposal were refused, any eventual strike would be declared illegal by the public authorities.

This communication was received with cries of "it's too late". While Mr. Prézeau called on the journalists present to bear witness to the unanimity of the workers, the workers opted to strike by a vote of raised hands. For the first time in forty years Montréal was going to be deprived of public transportation.

The local leaders of the Brotherhood had drafted a nine-point manifesto in which they laid down their conditions for returning to work. They demanded:

— The recognition of the Brotherhood as the only bargaining agent of the employees with the company;

— The closed shop, that is to say, the obligation of all the employees to be members of the Brotherhood and to pay it the required dues;

— The immediate payment of the profit-sharing bonuses provided for in the collective agreement of 1940;

— A general increase in salaries to make them equal to those of mass transit employees in Toronto (the only Canadian city which could be compared in that era to Montréal, and where the salaries were —and still are a quarter of a century later—higher than those of Montréal);

— No discrimination against the strikers;

— Softening of the disciplinary rules imposed on the employees;

— The final settlement of the mutual benevolent association "affair" to prevent application of the "bad" system which would shortly be submitted to the employees (The company wanted to change the rules of the mutual assurance system, which was paid for by the employees' contributions, to exclude sickness benefits and life insurance payments, and to retain only the retirement pensions);

— Salary readjustments in certain special cases; time-and-a-half after eight hours of work and double time after 12 hours of work; time-and-a-half on Sundays and holidays for the first eight days and double time for all additional work (Up to then time-and-a-quarter was given after 50 hours and time-and-a-half after 58 hours of work in one week);

— Paid vacations.

The Brotherhood would later assert that only the first four conditions were essential to the settlement. But on this March 28 evening in 1943, they all seemed vital to the strikers.

Mr. Marquette invited the union members to stay where they were, promising them that provisions would be brought to them. The members who were operating the streetcars that night were advised to return them to the garages and to get to the headquarters at the Atwater Market. The occupation of the Market began.

The strike hit the citizens like a blackjack in the early hours of Monday morning. Unless one had an emergency or was one of the privileged few, there was no question of taking taxis, which were expensive and increasingly rare due to the gasoline rationing imposed during the war. The Royal Automobile Club of Canada unsuccessfully called on the federal oil controller for a temporary suspension of the rationing. Thousands of workers and small salary-earners went to work on foot, often a distance of several miles. Others decided to stay home. Sometimes neighbours formed car pools to get to work. According to one daily, "one could also see... numerous trucks with human grapes clinging to them". Many schoolchildren played truant. Motorists took their revenge on Montreal Tramways, which liked to argue that private cars slowed down traffic in city streets, by showing that traffic was moving well despite the absence of the streetcars, and the increase in the number of cars.

The Montréal municipal police authorities, from the start of the strike, ordered all agents to be on the alert in case of incidents. But it soon appeared that the officers were not disposed to be overzealous, and a Montreal

Tramways spokesman complained about this on Monday morning.

Of course, Montreal Tramways tried to reestablish service, despite the conflict. Around ten thirty in the morning, the vice-president and general manager of the company, Mr. D.E. Blair, announced that if the police would offer a little more effective protection than what they had given up to then, an attempt would be made to put a few cars in operation. At noon, the spokesmen of Local 790 improved on this, saying that if at least one policeman were assigned to each car, its members would try to get the mass transit system going again that afternoon.

But these attempts were unsuccessful. In the morning a few employees tried to take some streetcars out of the Mount Royal garage, not knowing that the power had been cut off at the source by the strikers and that it was impossible to start the cars. A little before noon, nevertheless, a few streetcars were brought out of the Saint-Denis-Fleurimont garage, under a strong police escort, but the alerted strikers and their sympathizers showed up on the premises some 1,200 strong, and several lay down on the rails. There was no question of crossing this human barrier. After this incident, picket lines were set up at the entrances to all the garages.

The company called on the police to chase away the picketers, but the police refused, saying, according to the daily *Le Devoir* of March 29, "that peaceful picketing is legal". According to the same newspaper story, the company tried to convince the police that the strike itself was illegal, but "the police declared that it was not officially informed that the strike... was illegal".

The Montreal Chamber of Commerce protested against the strike to the federal government from the first day. It sent the Minister of Labour, Humphrey Mitchell, the following telegram: "The Montréal tramways strike is paralyzing all industry and commerce—We want all possible measures taken as soon as possible to reestablish the means of transport."

Montréal City Council, in the wake of serious financial difficulties in the local administration, was in that period powerless and under the trusteeship of an administrator named by the Québec government. But Council spokesmen nonetheless made known their views on the crisis.

Mayor Adhémar Raynault said that the strike was the responsibility of the federal authorities and that the City could do nothing about it. Mr. J. Omer Asselin, Chairman of the Executive Committee, a post which in normal times gave full authority over the internal administration of the city, declared that the City, conscious of the gravity of the situation, had communicated with the directors of Montreal Tramways to ask them to do everything in their power to settle the conflict as soon as possible. He too stressed that the City did not have jurisdiction in this matter.

Another elected municipal government official expressed a more categorical opinion. Alderman Jean-Marie Savignac — who would in his turn become Chairman of the Executive Committee — declared:

> "By going on strike, the tramways employees are using to the fullest a right conferred on them by federal law. And I hope that Ottawa is going to show as much sympathy and kindness to these employees striking in Québec as it has lately shown in the coal and steel strikes in the English provinces."

It was wartime. A very popular mayor was in an internment camp for having suggested to the populace that they evade military service. The perennial quarrel between English-speaking and French-speaking Canadians was reaching one of its periodic peaks. The strikers were indirectly referring to this in their demand for salaries comparable to those of their equivalents in Toronto, the metropolis of English Canada. Mr. Savignac stressed this in his turn, then continued:

> "The public owes it to itself to show its sympathy with these heads of families who are fighting for their existence. For no-one knows all the

employees have endured from the Company in the last two years. In pushing its employees to strike in this way, the tramway company surely has a hidden motive. Does it want to increase its fares to three tickets for 25 cents, or, even more, to weaken or destroy its employees' pension fund?"

The strikers received other, unexpected support from one of the unions that the Brotherhood was trying to dislodge, the Catholic union. The representative of the Montréal Tramways Employees' Union affiliated to the CCCL, Mr. J.-A. Chagnon, made the following declaration to the newspapers:

"To whom it may concern:

"The Tramways' Employees' Union has done its full duty in trying to prevent the present conflict. First, from July 1941, it called for the payment of the cost-of-living bonus and of the industrial bonus. It put into effect all peaceful means, overtures and requests with regard to the Company, the Regional Council, and an appeal to the National Council.

"The Union regrets to have to declare publicly that neither the Company, nor the councils, regional and national, have applied all the attention and diligence required to solve a problem of the importance of ours, whose multiple consequences are today apparent to all.

"Exasperated by the slowness and delays in the equitable settlement of their grievances, the tramway employees were at the end of their patience.

"The atmosphere was charged.

"The Canadian Brotherhood of Transport Employees played its game well. An unpardonable error by the bargaining committee which wanted to juggle a vote of confidence precipitated the events. The Brotherhood seized upon the occasion, and the strike broke out.

"Let us hope that things will not be spoiled further, that the interests of the tramway employee will be considered before the interests of Local 790, or those of the Brotherhood, and that justice will finally be rendered to this faithful servant of the public.

"The Tramways Union has never had any other preoccupation."

Meanwhile, in Ottawa, the Canadian Minister of Labour was declaring that never since the start of the war had a strike been declared with so little justification. Nevertheless, on the evening of the first day, he announced that he would send a mediator to Montréal, Mr. H. Carl Goldenberg, who in that period was one of the key civil servants assigned to the war effort. Mr. Goldenberg was given the powers of a federal arbitration board.

And like the housewife who continued to make a pie while the city burned down around her, Local 790, on March 29, the first day of the strike, held the referendum which had served as the pretext for the outbreak of the conflict. Its members voted by secret ballot between five in the morning and five in the evening, and once the votes were counted the president of the local, Mr. J.E. Beaudoin, announced that there were 1137 affirmative votes and 12 negative votes. He added, repeating his previous declarations, that his members were willing to assure streetcar service if only the police would help them.

At the strikers' headquarters in Atwater Market, the long vigil continued. Sandwiches by the tens of thousands were brought in from Lalumière Provisioning in the working-class neighbourhood of Saint-Henri, near the Market. Trucks full of white and chocolate milk were also ordered. Some strikers scarcely budged for three days from their little metal chairs, perched on the rough floor. They chatted; they waited for news; from time to time they stepped outside to get some fresh air, then went back inside. Certain strikers improvised shows. In the words of a witness: "We had magicians, we had singers, you could have made a movie with the employees..."

Outside it was business as usual. Mediator Goldenberg, after his appointment, made official contact in Ottawa with the general president of the Brotherhood, Mr. Mosher. The two men then went to Montréal. At Atwater Market the leader of the strikers, Paul-Émile Marquette, swore that if there had to be an agreement it would be signed there, in the Market, in the presence of the workers.

On Tuesday, the second morning of the strike, there were still plenty of pedestrians, but transportation was a little better organized than on the previous day. Most of the war industries, the public utilities companies and the big firms had set up a system to transport their employees by truck. The Royal Automobile Club reiterated its request to the oil controller to obtain a softening of the gasoline rationing, but received another refusal.

The big stores operated at a slower pace, with reduced personnel. The hospitals reported that about a quarter of their employees failed to check in. Courses were suspended in what was then the new building of the University of Montréal on Mount Royal Boulevard.

An unfounded rumor circulated that the City of Montréal would municipalize the Tramways Company. As for the Company, it did not succeed in putting a single streetcar line into operation.

The police, from a semblance of neutrality the previous day, now revealed themselves to be almost sympathetic to the strikers. To justify its refusal to escort employees who wanted to take the streetcars out, the police department told journalists, according to the account in *Le Devoir* of March 30, that it "is useless to expose the lives of policemen (to danger) and to turn the municipal police into an object of ridicule, when the strikers are more numerous than the police and the arms which they have available—passive resistance and picketing—are more effective than the means that can be used against them."

The same newspaper adds that: "The views held at municipal police headquarters are not exactly to the advantage of the Company. The declarations of the general manager of the Tramways Company are judged harshly there. It is even said that the present strike is the direct consequence of the policy that the company has followed for a number of years. Certain officers of the company are even blamed for being responsible for the strike, having too often in the past abused the good faith of the employees who have been grossly deceived."

However the *Montreal Star,* an English-language daily, attacked the strikers virulently the same day in an editorial. After discussing the causes of the strike, the commentator wrote:

"As an inevitable result, the tramways strike will cost the lives not only of many young Canadian soldiers on the ground, at sea and in the air, but also of many allied soldiers. The strike will affect all of Canada since the son of some mother in British Columbia will probably lose his life because airplanes were not produced in sufficient number. Some young man from the Maritimes will probably pay the ultimate price of negligence because submarines will not be effectively detected. Each hour and each day lost in no matter what war plant of this country can only have a destructive effect on the war effort of Canada. This is just what Hitler hopes for."

The *Montreal Star*'s editorial did not help the poor reporter of that daily who was following events at strike headquarters. He was abused, and some strikers allowed themselves the pleasure of breaking windows at the newspaper's building.

During Tuesday the federal conciliator, Mr. Goldenberg, increased his meetings with representatives of the company and the Brotherhood (led by Mr. Mosher). At the end of the day, a proposed agreement was concluded, in the presence of delegates of the company, the Brotherhood and the two other unions.

This agreement included four points. First, transportation services would be immediately reestablished. Second, there would be no discrimination against any employee whatsoever. Third, there would be new elections for a bargaining committee representative of the employees. Finally, the employees would decide by secret ballot, one week after the resumption of work, which union they wanted to represent them.

President Mosher submitted this proposed agreement to the strikers at the Atwater Market, early Tuesday evening. Nothing could be done. Unanimously, the strikers rejected an agreement which, to all intents and purposes, did not contain any answer to their demands.

When the negotiations resumed late in the evening and in the middle of the night, Mr. Mosher returned to the Market, announcing that he had obtained a satisfactory agreement, that the Brotherhood was recognized by the company. He spoke in English to the strikers, the majority of whom were French-speaking, and was warmly applauded. But when Paul-Émile Marquette translated the proposals of the president into French there was a chorus of boos.

The strikers were not happy either with the proposed settlement or, above all, with the fact that the Company directors and the federal mediator had not come to sign the agreement in their presence, at the Market, as Mr. Marquette had promised them the night before. There was even one worker who got up on the rostrum of the Market, climbed on the piano that was there, and shouted "that Blair (the general manager of the company) is going to come sign it in front of us, and we aren't going back as long as we haven't seen him."

It took four hours of debate, from three to seven in the morning, to convince the strikers to accept the settlement. Finally, Mr. Marquette told them that any worker who refused to return to work would have to take personal responsibility for his attitude. In spite of everything the members had confidence in Marquette and in Mosher. They agreed, and at daybreak on March 31 the agreement was accepted.

While waiting for the official signing of the agreement, the president of Montreal Tramways, Mr. R. N. Watts, made the following declaration to the press:

"We have accepted the recommendations of the federal Minister of Labour presented by Mr. Goldenberg. We have judged that war industries must be maintained at full production, and in order to do that, there is no doubt that easy transportation conditions must be reestablished immediately.

"We believe that the thousands of users of our company's cars ought to restore transportation, an indispensible service, as soon as possible. In these circumstances, given the recommendations of the Minister of Labour and given the fact that the Canadian Brotherhood has accepted these recommendations, we have deemed that the company also ought to accept them."

The maintenance workers got busy clearing the rails which had been unused for three days. The first tram left the Mount Royal garage at nine o'clock in the morning, and by late afternoon service was totally restored.

While the leaders of the company and the Brotherhood were getting ready for the official signing of the agreement, Local 790, learning that the Brotherhood would from then on be the recognized representative of the workers, threatened a general protest strike of all union members affiliated to the American Federation of Labour in the City of Montréal. The newspapers pointed out that if there were a general strike, the city would be put under martial law and occupied by troops. (The threat was not carried out).

On April 1, the full text of the agreement, which read as follows, was published:

1) Given the present war conditions and the responsibility of the interested parties to provide public transportation in Montréal and its suburbs, service will resume immediately.

2) The workers presently on strike agree to return to work immediately, and they will be allowed to do so without any discrimination being exercised against them.

3) Once the above-mentioned conditions have been fulfilled, the Company and the Canadian Brotherhood of Railway, Transport and General Workers

agree that the latter will have the right to at once designate three employees of the Company who will comprise a bargaining committee, and once these persons have been designated the Company agrees to recognize this committee as the sole bargaining agent of its employees. The committee thus formed will remain in operation until July 1, 1944, and its members will afterwards be elected each year by secret ballot. If, at any time after July 1, 1944, the Company has cause to believe that the bargaining committee does not represent the majority of its employees, the Brotherhood agrees to accept the holding of a secret vote, under the supervision of the federal Department of Labour, for the choice of a bargaining committee representative of the employees.

4) The Company and the bargaining committee must agree to discuss any change in the present contract between the Company and its employees which may be proposed by the Company or the bargaining committee, and if an agreement cannot be reached to satisfy a majority of the representatives of the Company and of the bargaining committee, it is agreed that any question not settled will be submitted to the decision of the National Wartime Labour Council or to any other agency that the federal government could create to this end. The Brotherhood commits itself that there will be no strike as long as all the recourses to the federal bodies created for the settlement of industrial conflicts have not been exhausted."

In sum, the Brotherhood was recognized by the Company; it could, through its representatives, discuss all the dispositions of the 1940 contract, but in the future, the right to strike of its members was severely limited.

But outside of the recognition of their union, the strikers had not obtained any tangible, immediate advantage. Many of them were frustrated. The conflict was not yet really settled, especially since it soon appeared that even the recognition of the Brotherhood was far from being total. It took more than two years, two other strikes and the threat of a third, and the temporary takeover of Montreal Tramways by the federal government, before the Brotherhood and the Company finally arrived at a truce.

In the days that followed the March strike, the Brotherhood designated its bargaining committee, made up of Messrs. Eucher Corbeil, Aimé Cardinal and Paul Valiquette. The first act of the committee was to appeal to the National Wartime Labour Council about the decision of its regional committee on the profit-sharing bonus.

While the Council was getting ready to hear the appeal, in May 1943, Local 790 and the Catholic union asserted that the Brotherhood did not have the right to make an appeal, since it had not participated in the signing of the agreement of 1940. The Council concluded from this, on May 19, that the status of the Brotherhood had not been clearly established; it ruled that the commissioner, Goldenberg, had exceeded his authority in proposing a strike settlement that did not have the assent of all the interested parties; it wondered if the change in representation — from Local 790 to the Brotherhood — had been done without recourse to fraud or coercion; finally, it asked the Minister of Labour to clearly indicate the real representatives of the tramway employees.

Five days after the publication of the decision, on May 25, 1943, the Minister of Labour informed the National Labour Council that Local 790 had withdrawn its objections and that the Catholic union had confirmed its previously declared intention to support the appeal lodged by the Brotherhood.

The Council then proceeded to examine the appeal, and on June 17 it ruled in favour of the Brotherhood: the profit-sharing bonus could in no way be likened to the cost-of-living bonuses covered by the Order-in-Council of 1941, and Montreal Tramways was bound to pay the employees the amounts owed, retroactive to January 1, 1942. The total amount of these bonuses reached $1,800,000, and the amount paid to individuals in certain cases went as high as $750.

This was a brilliant victory for the Brotherhood. Its credit among the employees grew correspondingly, but it still had not solidly established its credentials with the Company. Local 790 continued to recruit and organize the workers, and the Company gave one of its leaders an unpaid leave of absence and permission to recruit on the premises during working hours.

At the end of 1943 the local leaders of the Brotherhood presented the employer with demands for the alteration of the 1940 contract. The negotiations got under way very slowly. In early February 1944, the Company announced that it wanted to modify the mutual assurance system in force since 1903, to exclude sickness and death payments, and to retain only retirement pensions, while increasing the employees' contribution to the mutual fund. Despite the vigourous objections of the Brotherhood, which stressed the importance of studying the consequences of such a change at length, the employees were called to a meeting on February 9 where the changes were explained, and a vote on the question was taken on February 15. The modifications were rejected by about 95% of the employees.

A few days later, a new crisis broke out. The tension of the inter-union struggle between the Brotherhood and Local 790 had repercussions on the level of personal relations. Tramways conductors who were members of the Brotherhood were refusing to ride on the same streetcar with ticket takers who were members of Local 790. Three employees, members of the Brotherhood, were fired for refusing to work with colleagues who were members of the rival union.

Following these firings, the employees went out on a spontaneous strike on February 18, without the authorization of the leaders of the Brotherhood. The firings had been the straw that broke the camel's back. The employees were also irritated with the slowness of the negotiations, and with the fact that their salaries were frozen at the 1940 rate while salaries were higher in the war industries around them. The increase in the volume of transportation was also leading to more overtime, still paid at lower rates than prevailed elsewhere.

The strike only lasted 36 hours, but local leaders of the Brotherhood had to threaten to resign to convince the employees to return to work. The workers went back, but the members of the Brotherhood were more insistent than ever on full recognition of their union. Two conciliators, Mr. Cyprien Miron of the Québec Department of Labour and Mr. Bernard Wilson, of the Federal Department of Labour, were charged with studying the causes of the conflicts. They made a report in April, concluding that the ambiguity of management-labour relations and the inter-union conflict had caused the strike.

But earlier, in February, the federal government had adopted new labour legislation, which applied particularly to transportation and communications. It set the conditions under which a union could be recognized as representing a group of employees and gave a recognized union the right to require that the employer negotiate with it.

Standing on this legislation, the Brotherhood asked the National Labour Council for recognition of itself as the representative of the tramway employees. It received its official recognition on April 13, 1944, which permitted it to speed up the negotiations with the Company.

But these negotiations snagged on one point: the Brotherhood was demanding a complete union shop, which would oblige all the employees to be dues-paying members of the Brotherhood.

Conciliators and conciliation boards named by the government followed one after another during the spring and summer without being able to bridge the chasm that separated the Company and the union on the issue of the union shop.

At the end of July the Brotherhood held a strike vote among its members, who cast 3,520 affirmative votes and 78 negative ones. The text on the ballot summed up the situation. Here is the gist of it:

The question in dispute between Montreal Tramways and your committee, on which it has not been possible to arrive at a satisfactory settlement, touches on a union shop clause to be added to the collective agreement regulating working conditions.

Your committee insists on obtaining the inclusion of the following clause in the contract: "No employee occupying a function covered by the content of this agreement will be retained in the employ of the Company for a period of more than thirty days, unless he is a member in good standing of the Brotherhood. This clause must not be applied in such a manner as to infringe on the rights of employees as defined in the Law on Reinstatement in a Civil Job, Statutes of Canada 6-7, George VI, Chapter 31."

The Company refuses to accept the said clause or to propose a compromise which would be acceptable to your committee. A conciliation commission created by the federal Department of Labour, which has tried to bring about a settlement of the conflict, has pronounced itself in its report to the Minister against the closed shop clause proposed by your committee. The said report added, however, that a majority of the members of the Commission were favourable to the principle of the closed shop, but did not succeed in reaching an agreement on the formulation to propose.

It becomes evident that the Company will not willingly accept the union shop clause proposed by your committee and that such a disposition, if it could be obtained in some way, will have to be obtained by the collective withdrawal of the services of the employees as long as the dispute is not settled.

Given the circumstances described hereinabove, you are asked to indicate, by marking one of the spaces provided lower down with an "X", whether or not you favour recourse to a strike with the aim of forcing the Company to accept the union shop in the modified contract. It is understood that a vote favourable to the strike will signify your firm resolution to participate in a strike at the time that will be set by the undersigned committee, and a vote against the strike will authorize the said committee to conclude with the Company the most satisfactory agreement possible under the circumstances.

The ballot was signed by Messrs. Corbeil, Cardinal and Valiquette, respectively president, vice-president and secretary of the bargaining committee.

On August 1, the leaders of the Brotherhood advised the Company of the result of the vote, and at midnight on August 2, public transportation in Montréal was again paralyzed by a strike.

The strikers this time did not enjoy all the sympathy which had been given them 16 months earlier during the first conflict. A strike to obtain union recognition is not too popular in any era, and even less in wartime. But the strikers held fast.

On Friday, August 11, on the tenth day of the strike, the federal government intervened, under the War Measures Act, and named two controllers who took responsibility for the administration of Montreal Tramways. These controllers were Mr. E. L. Cousins, wartime administrator of the Canadian Atlantic ports, and Mr. J. E. Saint-Laurent, vice-president of the National Ports Council.

The Order-in-Council (P.C. 6416) designating the controllers also ordered the employees to return to work on Monday, August 14, and to pursue negotiations with the Company until the conclusion of an agreement. Meanwhile, the working conditions which existed before the strike were maintained.

When work resumed, so did the negotiations. The first collective agreement between Montreal Tramways and the Brotherhood was not concluded, however, until May 31, 1945, after several conciliation efforts and a new strike threat.

The contract which was finally signed did not provide for a complete union shop, but it recognized the

Brotherhood as the sole representative of the employees, guaranteed it information on any new employee, gave it exclusive rights to post union notices on company property, and obliged the Company to deduct union dues from the wages of any employee who signed an authorization to this effect.

As for the other working conditions, they could be considered exemplary for that era.

chapter six

the sky will be red hot

The City of Montréal was going through a difficult period. Mayor Camillien Houde had been imprisoned in an internment camp for encouraging people to resist conscription. The city, bled financially by the expenses of the Depression period and prevented by Québec from imposing an income tax, had fallen under the trusteeship of the provincial government in May 1940. An administrator, Honoré Parent, took control of all the affairs of the municipality. One of the effects of his rule was to considerably reduce the powers which city councillors had previously held over city employees.

These employees usually got their jobs through political favouritism. They might have thought themselves happy during the Depression, when their regular employment made them privileged compared to the thousands of unemployed. But with the coming of the war, the working conditions in the surrounding milieu improved, and the municipal employees, because of provincial trusteeship, could no longer even hope for the special favours of this or that councillor.

The workers of Montréal and of Québec in general were in a state of agitation. Perhaps they were particularly impressed by the action of the tramway employees, a group which resembled them in many respects. Moreover, Paul-Émile Marquette, who had sprung from the ranks of the tramway employees and now was regional organizer for the Canadian Congress of Labour, was doing union organizing among them.

The first workers to make a move were those known as "manuals": the workers assigned to the municipal incinerator, the sewer workers, and the workers on the aqueduct, in the parks, on public works and in the roads department. They were not young men — employment had been frozen during the Depression, and afterwards, the city's financial difficulties had reduced hiring possibilities.

In the spring of 1943, the workers began en masse to join a union affiliated to the Canadian Congress of Labour, the Canadian Brotherhood of Municipal Employees. Some workers who participated in union organizing at that time assert that department heads and foremen tried to form a rival union at the same time, but without success. In any case, the documents make no mention of such an attempt.

Towards mid-August, the City fired four employees — because of their union activities, according to the Brotherhood. The employees got together and threatened to stop work if these four workers were not rehired. Instead of receiving an answer from the City, they learned on August 20 that a fifth employee had been fired.

On Friday evening, August 20, the employees got together again, and decided to go out on strike, starting at midnight. Some 2,000 workers participated in the work stoppage, but the union agreed to take special measures to assure the maintenance of the aqueduct and not to deprive the city of water.

On Saturday morning all the workers were called to a mass meeting at the Assistance Publique hall on Lagauchetière Street to hear the reasons for the strike explained.

That morning, the city foremen tried to take trucks out of some garages, with the assistance of workers who had showed up for work either because they were not informed about the strike order, or because they didn't accept it.

Garbage was normally collected on Saturday, and skipping a collection in mid-August inevitably meant a nauseating stench in the city. The hospitals and the few big hotels out pressure on the City to get the garbage collected.

In the words of a striker of the period, "the big foremen tried to organize themselves with some strike-breakers to go back with private trucks... to the municipal shops. G. tried to get some men in, and there was a little bit of shoving around. But to say that the strike was hard, no, because the unity among the workers was too strong. Aside from that, people in the street were saying: they're doing the right thing, because of the salary they're getting compared to the salaries elsewhere in the other firms. We had the sympathy of the population; when you have that it's easy... if private trucks came, we let the air out of their tires..."

At the assembly on Saturday morning, the leaders of the local made it clear that the workers would go back to work on condition that the five fired workers be rehired and that the City also make other concessions: the union shop, the full cost-of-living bonus of $4.25 a week retroactive to March 1, 1943, the closing of the public baths on Sundays and the promise to negotiate a collective agreement with the Brotherhood.

"At that time there was a funny situation," a witness recalls. "The Canadian Congress of Labour, which was under the presidency of (A.R.) Mosher, in Ottawa, had promised the government in power not to go on strike during the war. But we didn't worry about that; we went on strike anyway. So then, right away — it was a Sunday — we got a telegram from Ottawa telling us to go back to work.

"There were three of us (on the strike committee); we met with (Guy Merril) Desaulniers who was the lawyer of the Canadian Congress in Montréal at that time; he was beginning; he was very young... he called us over to his private house, and we talked about it there. They said: 'What are you doing?' Well I said: 'Do it, go back if you want; me, I'm not going back.' And when they saw that I really meant it, and that I had the support of the men at that moment, they decided to continue the strike. The next day about ten o'clock in the morning, we got a telegram from Québec (telling us) that they were sending someone to meet with us. It was the Deputy Minister of Labour, (O'Connell) Maher."

Monday morning, the city became aware of the fact that the garbage had not been collected on Saturday. Some streets were lined with garbage cans, wooden and cardboard boxes. Sometimes the cans had been overturned and their contents scattered over the sidewalk or the street. It was very hot, and the odours were disagreeable.

City councillors went to City Hall to get information on the conflict. They knew that the executive committee of the city could not do anything, that all the authority with respect to hiring and firing of personnel was vested in the Municipal Commission. An unidentified member of the executive declared to a journalist that the difficulties the City was facing with its workers were not surprising, "when discontented employees are not able to present their grievances to the competent authorities, obliged as they are to go through their immediate superiors."

From all the evidence, some of the municipal politicians regretted the passing of the happy era in which they had a direct authority over personnel. Perhaps, when everything was taken into consideration, some employees regretted it also, since to a certain extent they had fallen out of the frying pan into the fire. The foremen were the petty kings now, with full control over hiring and firing.

But on Monday, the third day of the strike, nobody was asking the opinion of the foremen. The administrator delegated by Québec to run the affairs of the city, Mr. Honoré Parent, went into conference at about eleven o'clock in the morning with the president of the Municipal Affairs Commission, Mr. L.-E. Potvin, the latter's deputy, Mr. L.-A. Lapointe, the director of the city's public works service, Mr. H.-A. Gibeau, and a few other service directors.

During the afternoon, Mr. Gibeau made the following statement to the press:

> "It should be remembered that the municipal employees fulfill a public function.

"According to the law, the department heads are responsible for the administration of their services. The department heads name and replace their subordinates, with the approval of the competent authority.

"In the present case, we have dismissed from their functions five employees who were remiss in their duty. They were dismissed for cause, on the recommendation of their immediate superior. A simple disciplinary measure is involved.

"It is for this reason alone that a group of our employees have imposed a strike, at the instigation of an outside labour organization.

"Furthermore, on Saturday morning and today as well, the majority of our employees returned to their work, but were prevented from resuming their tasks due to threats proferred by certain strike leaders.

"Even today, at least six cars and trucks, some of them coming from the outside and filled with agitators, drove around the city in order to stop our workers from accomplishing their work.

"As we have already stated in other circumstances, we have always discussed working conditions with our personnel and we have succeeded in satisfying them on the basis of the funds which we had at our disposal.

"Since September 6, 1940, we have established stipend and salary scales, regulated working conditions and improved the lot of our employees to a considerable extent.

"On several occasions they have given us testimony of their gratitude for this. Particularly insofar as the manual employees of the Incinerator and the Roads Department are concerned, we have remained in continual contact with their representatives. We have always taken their demands into consideration. All our conversations, up to now, have produced happy results.

"On September 18 and 19, 1942, our employees elected representatives with whom we have dealt up to now. After discussions with these gentlemen and numerous deliberations, the competent authority, in order to meet with their wishes, has enacted the following:

"It recognizes the existence of a grievance committee in the public ways division, street maintenance and incineration section, made up of the six delegates that these sections elected September 18 and 19, 1942."

Among other things this committee had the duty of:

"submitting to the public works service director the grievances that the personnel in general could have relating to their working conditions;

"submitting to the interested foreman and to higher authorities the grievances that any such employee or group of employees could have."

"These are the conditions existing between the employees and ourselves. We have always respected them up to now, and so have they. Furthermore, on October 28, 1942, salary increases were granted and new working conditions were consented to, retroactive to the preceding October 1. Since then, other salary increases have been granted and the working conditions have been further improved.

"In the present case, the instigators of the strike have not followed the above-mentioned procedure. They have not even observed the law. First of all they threatened the municipality with a strike because the four above-mentioned employees were going to be fired by the persons in charge of the municipal workshops division. The name of a fifth person dismissed from his functions has since been added.

"These employees have been dismissed for cause, as we have already said, at the request of their immediate superior.

"We have no objection to revealing the reasons for these dismissals. We have never had objections either to the submission of the case of these employees to the above-mentioned grievance committee, or to the creation of a grievance committee for the municipal workshops' employees' division, after these workers have resumed their work, if they desire to name representatives as the incinerator and roads department employees have done.

"We want to discuss directly with our employees, and the proof that they are well treated is that their grievance, up to now, for going on strike, is the dismissal of the men mentioned previously, as the resolution adopted on July 30 by a certain group clearly shows.

"It is evident that what is involved here is a union that is seeking to implant itself in City Hall and to prevent our employees from freely attending to their duties. Moreover, this strike is illegal. As Judge Cloutier declared in his judgment relating to the case of David Côté:

> "By what right and in virtue of what principle, I ask myself without, however, being able to find the answer, could one presume in this way to establish a line of men to hinder the freedom to return to work and to thus deprive of their earnings those workers who did not want to remain in illegality but who, on the contrary, were of the opinion that the demands ought to be judged on their merit in the atmosphere, the order and the conditions provided for by the law. These wars of prestige in no way rest on the right of association. They constitute modes of exercise, or rather of abuse, of this right, which converge on its negation much more than on its principle and the real interests of the workers."

(end of the quotation from the judge)

"There is no authority possible in our different services if our superintendants and the director of public works are not readily able to dismiss employees whom they no longer need or who do not do their duty. It is up to the competent authority to discuss these cases.

"In consequence, we invite all our employees to resume work on Wednesday morning, at eight o'clock, or sooner if it is their desire.

"Starting on next Wednesday, August 25, all our employees who have not presented themselves to resume their work... will be considered as having resigned.

"It goes without saying that we assure all possible protection to those persons who resume their work."

Despite this ultimatum from the City and the firm intention it expressed of not ceding any management powers to the union, the strikers held fast. Moreover, during Monday, they received support from other unions, particularly from the transit employees and shipyard workers, who were also affiliated to the Canadian Congress of Labour. A spokesman for the CCL announced that there would be union meetings on Wednesday for the city firemen and policemen, but hastened to add that there was no question of their going on strike. Their meeting would simply be part of the organizing campaign started three months earlier.

On Tuesday Mr. Aimé Laurin, president of the local of the Brotherhood of Municipal Employees, declared that not only was there no question of ending the strike, despite the ultimatum of the director of public works, but that this ultimatum had so displeased the strikers that the union was having a hard time persuading them to maintain essential services at the aqueduct.

But late Tuesday afternoon, the negotiations aimed at settling the conflict got under way seriously. The president of the Québec Municipal Affairs Commission conferred during the afternoon with the administrator delegated to Montréal, Mr. Parent, and in the evening he met with the secretary of the Minister of Labour, Mr.

J. O'Connell-Maher. The latter also held talks with the representatives of the strikers.

"Honoré Parent had sworn not to meet with us," says one of the leaders of the strikers in that period. "He had said that he would not meet us for any reason. That's why they decided to send us Maher... He asked us for our demands. The first thing that we asked for was to be recognized. The city said: Never. They didn't want to have a union because it would have been a pack of trouble. For an employer this was perhaps right, but the workers were twice as right. But they recognized us; they were obliged to recognize us because of the circumstances."

From the Tuesday talks, a settlement finally emerged. Around ten o'clock, the president of the Municipal Affairs Commission, Mr. Potvin, announced that the Commission had decided to ask the provincial Ministry of Labour to set up an arbitration board to settle the dispute. At midnight the strikers lifted the picket lines in front of the municipal buildings.

But the agreement still had to be ratified. The strikers were called together on Wednesday morning at ten o'clock at the Assistance Publique hall. There were a few who were recalcitrant, but the majority ratified the proposed agreement: an arbitration board would be made up of a representative of the City, one from the Brotherhood and a president chosen by the first two. The five fired employees would not be able to resume work until the board handed down a ruling, but while waiting they would receive their salaries from the City.

The workers resumed work at two o'clock Wednesday afternoon. Only some 150 of them had showed up that morning to respect the ultimatum issued on Monday by the director of public works. Moreover, the Municipal Commission had put off the deadline set in the ultimatum from eight in the morning to one in the afternoon.

Temporarily, the conflict was settled.

But less than four months later, the workers stopped work again, this time to support a strike by the city's firemen and policemen. Although each of the two groups had had a more or less steady association representing them for several decades, they had begun serious organization within the Canadian Congress of Labour, at the instigation of Paul-Émile Marquette. This was in the spring of 1943, around the time of the first tramways strike. The firemen were the first to get involved; then the policemen joined them in calling for a single charter from the CCL. It was mentioned earlier that, at the time of the first strike by the city employees, a spokesman for the policemen and firemen had hastened to exclude the possibility of a sympathy strike. But later their time came too.

Working conditions were not easy. As Mr. Roger Lavigueur, one of the directors of the 1943 strike, explained it: "I entered the police service on October 1, 1936 as a cadet, and in this period we had a salary of $250 per year, which immediately marked us to be revolutionaries in the police service."

"We had to report to our officer at six o'clock every day to finish our work at seven o'clock the next morning," he continued, recalling his first years of service. "And the following day we started again at six o'clock to finish at eight o'clock. In that time we did three hours inside, three hours outside, but the time that we were working outside on reserve we were always subject to calls for fires, for murders, we were always subject to recall during our rest periods, and we had to take our meal hours within those periods. All that made us do about a hundred hours of work per week without remuneration for overtime, and one holiday for each fifteen days; we calculated that a policeman lived twenty years in the station and five years at home."

Nevertheless, conditions had changed a little by 1943. There was a 48-hour week and the maximum salary was as high as $1,800 a year. But "we didn't have any right to discuss working conditions, we couldn't make ourselves heard, we couldn't present grievances, we could only accept the good will of our employer, and by employer I mean the City authorities as well as the police force. We were completely their slaves."

The policemen had formed a union once before, in 1919. It had lasted two years. There were so many reprisals that the policemen had lived in fear for the next quarter of a century. The only organizations they had before the union of 1943 were a sporting association, which let them participate in police force athletic contests, and a benevolent and retirement association which was presided over by the big boss, the chief of police himself.

The union organization drive of 1943 took its first steps under the camouflage of a sporting club. There were 467 members signed up within the space of a month and a half. Mr. Lavigueur explained how he told his early colleagues: "Well then guys, if we don't succeed in getting more than ten policemen each we run a chance of all being fired, but if we get ten men each in three days, that will make 300 or 400 — they aren't going to put 400 policemen outside."

Nobody sold out. The first group to get organized were the motorcyclists, "and the motorcyclists, like today, are a rather enthusiastic category of policemen... if you were one of them you didn't talk. You kept quiet. It was almost a matter of life or death then."

Not without humour Mr. Lavigueur related that at the end of about a month and a half the police director saw what was happening and had a letter circulated denouncing the sporting club as an attempt at union organization, which was totally forbidden, and threatening reprisals: "That letter helped us enormously. With its aid we put ourselves in motion more openly and we asked for the help of the Canadian Congress of Labour."

The firemen had come to the CCL at about the same time, or perhaps a little earlier, by a different route.

In 1919 the firemen had also formed a union and had engaged in a one-day strike. At that time the City had promised to settle all their grievances if they went back to work. According to Mr. Armand Vanasse, who was president of the union of 1943, "They went back to their duties, and then what I have been told is that the authorities did not keep their word, and that furnished us with an experience, so that when we went on strike we said: 'We are not on strike to get salaries, we are not on strike

111

for working conditions, we are on strike for the recognition of a union'."

Mr. Vanasse entered the service of the city as a fireman in 1931, "to work 84 hours a week, which meant every day of the week, day or night, to make an average of 84 hours. Every second Sunday we had to work from eight in the morning to eight o'clock Monday morning. We had six days of ten hours, and when you got to Sunday, 24 hours, that made 84 hours. And then you went home Monday morning and you went back Monday night, and you did six nights of 14 hours, which again makes 84 hours. So that's all the time you had with your family, except for the annual vacations. There were no days off or anything else like that."

As for salaries, "I started at $1,400 and the maximum I could reach was $1,800 as an ordinary fireman. It went on like that up to the start of the war; then, in 1940 I believe, we were given a cost-of-living bonus of $104, added to the $1,800, and then that stayed the same; we went into 1943 with the same thing. At that time I had 12 or 13 years of service and I was earning exactly $1,904 per year to live on."

As for the hiring conditions, one had to be strong, and to be "a good smoke-eater", to have "the capacity to take plenty of smoke without falling down."

"And there was this pride that wasn't good. In a given district — they were always called districts — the person who was responsible for the station — he was called the "branchier", the division chief — the guy from the particular station where there was a fire, he wanted to be the first there and put out the fire himself. He didn't want the guy from the neighbouring station to put out the fire for him. That meant that one made tremendous physical efforts. (The firemen) affected their health in pushing like that, in breathing all sorts of gases and then making superhuman efforts, because they normally could have withdrawn and let someone else go in, but no, this was a matter of pride, this was sacred. Mustn't have help from the others. The district chiefs hesitated to ask for help. They let people work and tire themselves out so that nobody could say: 'Look at that, he can't put out his fires'."

At the station house there was maintenance work, "and then after, people used to say we played cards — that was a bit true — but also sometimes we formed groups, complained about our situation, and all those things existed in all the stations. And there were also what were called the station lawyers, people who saw a lot of other things, but I can't go into a lot of details..."

Were fires frequent? "In the popular language, you know, you don't do statistics; that would be rather silly... it was the custom to say that we had to have our quota of fires each year. It was like raising families. We used to say, we have to have our quota; if we don't have it in the fall, we'll have it in the spring, early in the spring. Sometimes, like today, we had nice periods, long periods when we didn't have fires.

"At that time we also had brush fires, those famous brush fires. Because the periphery wasn't built up, there were plenty of big fields, and in the spring the children took a malicious pleasure in setting the grass on fire. We had to go put them out. Plenty of firemen didn't like having themselves called brushfire firemen. They wanted to work in the city, downtown, because it was the best firemen who worked in the city..."

In 1940 the firemen did not have an organization worth speaking of. According to Mr. André Plante, who was secretary of the union created in 1943, "the firemen had an independent union... it negotiated, it obtained a pair of boots, two more ties, it got increases of $60 for the old guys, $40 for the young guys, for two or three years. There was no question of a collective agreement; they received us when they felt like it; we were absolutely ignored... We were in total darkness for about thirteen years, from 1930 to 1943."

Says Mr. Vanasse: "There was merely a little union, which was said to be a company union in plain language, and the representatives, despite all their good intentions, could not meet the municipal authorities without having the permission of the fire chief, and when they arrived at City Hall, well, they always arrived too late — the budget was exhausted and there couldn't be salary increases. And that went on all the time, so much so that in the Forties, if I recall correctly, we had come to have a union that was only worth it when you died. If you died in service, you received $800 — to sum it up, we had come to have insurance on death rather than insurance on life."

The firemen had seen the action of the tramway employees; some of them had contacts with Paul-Émile Marquette, "the big manitou of the Canadian Congress of Labour at that time".

"The firemen began to organize themselves early in 1943; I believe it was in the month of March," relates Mr. Vanasse. "It started with meetings in cellars almost everywhere, in secret — it was necessary that this wouldn't be found out because it was deadly for a firemen's job."

They elected leaders; they began to collect union dues. "During this process the policemen, having got wind of the situation, also wanted to organize. The manual employees (of the city) were organized and they had gone on strike with the same Canadian Congress of Labour. Thus the policemen, not having had the time to do their organizing, set out with us to get union recognition, with the same documentation, I could say."

In the face of this rising wave the municipal authorities, more specifically the Municipal Affairs Commission, decided to submit the problem of the representation of all these groups (policemen, firemen, workers, and also office employees who would enter the picture later) to the ruling of an arbitration board. The board, headed by Mr. Roger Brossard, concluded that it was necessary to recognize those unions which had been formed. But the administrator delegated by Québec to the City of Montréal, Mr. Honoré Parent, did not agree. He proposed to the policemen and firemen that he would grant them the working conditions enjoyed by their colleagues in the City of Toronto (which for Montréal signified average pay increases of $500), but without recognizing their union.

On Monday, December 13, 1943, firemen, police-men and workers of the City of Montréal served the municipal authorities with an ultimatum: their unions had to be recognized before eleven o'clock in the morning of the next day, December 14, or there would be a strike.

The presidents of the three unions—policemen, firemen and workers—had arranged among themselves for a meeting at eleven o'clock in the morning on the 14th at the Assistance Publique hall on Lagauchetière Street. Members of the different unions were there also, awaiting the news. Mr. Paul-Émile Marquette was at City Hall, waiting for a last minute change of heart by the municipal authorities.

In fact, the policemen from the night patrol were at the Assistance Publique hall from the end of their shift, at seven o'clock in the morning. They were waiting for the strike order. "It was," said Mr. Lavigueur, "a group on the Force on which we were not counting at that moment; it was the group which had always voted against us, against the principle of the union, because in fact the working conditions in that sector, particularly the salaries, were very good. Seeing such a large group of detectives there gave me the hope that we would be successful."

"During that period," said Mr. Lavigueur, "we had in each of the police stations an apparatus that we called a gong, that is, a clock, that rang each time the firemen went out. We wanted to get control of that famous clock to give at least eleven rings to show the strike was on at eleven o'clock in the morning. The city au-thorities had found out that we were preparing to use the gong, but on the other hand we had found out a secret enough way to ring it without anybody being able to see who was ringing it. And at the strike of eleven the eleven rings sounded and the city went to great trouble to find out where the alarm ringer was. We had succeeded; the city had been had."

Even if the leaders of the Canadian Congress of Labour waited until eleven forty-five before declaring that their ultimatum had not been respected, the strike began at eleven o'clock. At two o'clock in the afternoon it was being observed by about three quarters of the policemen, firemen and workers.

The policemen and firemen on strike formed teams, and so that nothing would compromise relations in the future, groups of striking firemen went to "empty" the police stations, and the striking policemen did the same thing in the fire stations.

The strikers also organized emergency teams, although certain more militant strikers among the firemen employed themselves in sabotaging the emergency equipment.

The army was immediately put on alert. The policemen's president, Mr. Lavigueur, received a call during the day from a garage worker informing him that there were about three hundred RCMP agents in the garage, getting ready to go out on patrol with the cars of the striking municipal policemen.

Mr. Lavigueur sent a patrol of strikers onto the premises, at the corner of St-Vallier and Fleurimont, to see what was happening. "And on arriving on the premises," he related, "the vice-president (of the union) who was responsible for the patrol, saw that the first vehicles were arriving on Fleurimont Street. There were five of them in the car. Before the RCMP agents had time to do anything, the strikers had succeeded in taking away wires and spark-plugs, had succeeded in wrecking at least one radiator and in turning one car in the directtion opposite to where it was supposed to go.

"And then he gave me an urgent call to tell me it was true, there were three hundred men. I went back to the microphone (in the Assistance Publique hall) and ordered the whole hall to go to the Fleurimont site to stop the vehicles from going back on the road and thus breaking the strike.

"Getting to that place, we were perhaps more than 1,500. There was an inspector there—I remember the name very well, Inspector Poudrette — who was responsible at the time. I asked him who had given that order. He told me: 'I received the order to come here from Mr. Harvison'—who was the Commissioner of the Royal Canadian Mounted Police.

"I asked Inspector Poudrette to please telephone his boss. He called Inspector Harvison and I talked with him. I asked him who gave him the order. He told me: 'I received it by telegram, from the Minister of Justice, Mr. Louis Saint-Laurent.'

"I said: 'Would there be a possibility of immediately obtaining a copy of your order?' He replied that I would have it by telegram the next morning. I said: 'Sir, it's not a big thing, but can I rely above all on your honour and on your oath of office as a policeman that you really had an order'. He answered: 'Yes, sir.'

"I told him: 'I can tell you one thing. If this is a falsehood, you know that we are all armed and tomorrow, YOU CAN BE SURE THAT TOMORROW THE SKY WILL BE RED HOT.'

"We were all armed and we also knew that the army had sent troops into the western part of the city, and that another group that was sympathetic to our cause was stationed in Longueuil. We had certainly made use of the vote which was going on around that time — the yes or no vote on conscription, and that could have developed, in my opinion, into a civil war."

Otherwise there were few incidents. A union leader of the period asserts that there was not a single theft or a single major fire, adding: "Providence was on our side." There would have been an attempted car theft at the corner of Saint-Laurent and Laurier streets, but according to Mr. Lavigueur: "I can't tell you what happened... policemen in plainclothes took care of it; apparently the guy wasn't interested in stealing cars afterwards."

The policemen could count on the sympathy of other police forces. The policemen of the City of Outremont officially expressed their support.

And the strike continued. Because of the situation the regulator of electricity, Mr. H.J. Symington, lifted the curfew which plunged Montréal into darkness every evening during the war.

In the Assistance Publique hall where the strikers were staying, there were amateur contests; there was singing, dancing and story telling. In the words of a witness, "one could say we had a tremendous time." But the strike leaders were hoping that a settlement would come quickly "because there was danger that control would be lost... and then there would certainly be damage." Some members of the provincial Legislative Assembly showed up at the strike headquarters: Messers. Claude Jodoin, J.-A. Francoeur, Maurice Hartt, Paul Gauthier and Émile Boucher. Mr. Francoeur especially, because he was from the government party, was asked to intercede with Liberal Premier Adélard Godbout to make the Municipal Affairs Commission listen to reason.

At the deserted municipal police headquarters, the chief of police, Mr. Fernand Dufresne, was juggling the situation. He confided to reporters through indirect routes that he was beginning to be fed up with the refusal of the municipal authorities to hear the representations that he was making to them in the name of "his" men, and with his inability to deal directly with the men, forced as he was to always go through the administrator delegated by Québec, Mr. Parent. If one takes everything into account, his term as chief of police had been a difficult one: first the Depression, then the War, and to top it off, a general strike. During his term of office the population of Montréal had more than doubled, but the police force, from 1,396 members when he took power, had gone down to 1,395.

The strikers continued to wait. The presidents of the three unions — workers, firemen and policemen — had made "what was called a three musketeers agreement," Mr. Lavigueur related. "We had made an oath with the hands of the three joined, an oath on our honour that we would never give the order to our personnel to go back to work if all three did not go back. Before the walkout we were sure enough of the game that the City wanted to play, that it would certainly recognize the public works union, because it had done so in the past, and would also afterwards recognize the firemen, but would leave the policemen aside. And the City followed that tactic exactly—it recognized the unions of the manual workers and the firemen, and always refused to recognize the police union, until we succeeded in defeating them."

There was also the support of the tramway employees, whose union leaders went to the strike headquarters to declare that if they were needed the streetcar men would stop work too to help the city employees.

The talks between the municipal authorities and the provincial authorities were going on briskly. Mr. Lavigueur said he remembered that the strikers regularly saw "arriving in our hall a representative of the City, a member of the firemen's general staff, who came to bring messages in a little red car. Each time that there was a concession by the city, he came to bring the message... The acceptance of the public works union, that was one trip. After that the firemen's union—another trip. After that, another trip to tell of the refusal to recognize the police. And then, around six or seven o'clock, the temperature of the hall started to go up."

The agreement of the City to recognize the firemen's union was given verbally at first. The president of the union demanded a written and duly stamped confirmation. He received it. But there were still the policemen.

According to witnesses of the period, it was the Liberal deputy, J.-A. Francoeur, at the request of the strikers, who intervened with Premier Adélard Godbout to get him to intervene in turn with the Municipal Affairs Commission. At any rate, in the late evening, the policemen's union was also recognized. At two o'clock in the morning on December 15, the strike officially came to an end, after having lasted a little more than fourteen hours.

The Municipal Affairs Commission, through its president, L.-E. Potvin, announced the next day that it had asked the Québec Minister of Labour to set up arbitration commissions to study the salary demands of the employees in the Montréal public works, police and fire services. To those who were surprised at the extension of the settlement to salary demands, which had not been in question at the start of the strike, Mr. Potvin declared that he had learned of the intention of the three groups to present such demands in the near future, and that he hoped to settle all the grievances at the same time.

The ruling that followed the arbitration presided over by Mr. Roger Brossard granted the firemen and policemen conditions that were approximately equivalent to those of their Toronto colleagues. The firemen's schedules were reduced from 84 to 78 hours a week, and the maximum salary was raised from $1,800 to $2,400. The maximum salary for policemen was raised from $500 to $2,300 for a 48-hour week.

And so, in 1943, only the clerks and other office employees of the city had not gone on strike. Their turn came one week after the strike by the policemen, firemen and workers, on December 21. Their conflict was the longest; it lasted three weeks, until January 12, 1944.

Unlike the other groups, the white collar workers were not affiliated to the Canadian Congress of Labour, but rather to the Catholic unions, the Canadian and Catholic Confederation of Labour. The CCCL strikers, because of the rivalries between their organization and the CCL, and because of their absence from the general strike of December 14, did not get tangible support from the Montréal public service employees' groups who had preceded them in combat.

The civil service in that era had a bad reputation, because it was considered to be a nest of "patronage", of political favouritism. This was true not only of the municipality but also of the provincial and federal governments. In the words of a witness of the period, "to a large extent this was true because those who were able to get in (to the bureaucracy) had to make a series of overtures almost as important as the ones necessary for a candidate to the Académie Française. Once inside, they were generally given a task that wasn't too important, but with promises of promotions etc. for the future. These promises were rarely kept because once he had been placed the employee would be told: 'Listen, you asked for a job;

you have it; wait; promotions can't be given out just like that for nothing'."

"There were those who could rot all their lives in a secondary position," the same witness went on, "and who without a doubt had been happy to get into the civil service at the beginning, but who were realizing that this wasn't settling their problem at all and who were really rather frustrated."

The salaries in that era varied between about $900 and $2,500 per year. They had scarcely budged since the start of the war, while the cost of living had risen sharply. The recourses that the governments provided for the workers who wanted to improve their lot during the war did not apply to government employees.

A municipal civil servants' union had been set up a little before the war; it had taken a few steps which, though laudable, had produced few results. "Each year we submitted a memorandum to the municipal authorities, a sort of notebook of complaints, written with plenty of respect for authority," says a witness. Despite this docility, the city, in 1943, had reduced the annual pay of one of the union leaders by $300, giving lack of funds as an excuse.

The union presented the city with a grievance about this pay reduction, the first grievance which was settled to the satisfaction of the employees.

The dearth of concrete results obtained by the Catholic union of municipal civil servants had encouraged certain civil servants to turn to the Canadian Congress of Labour, the organization which seemed to be so successful for the tramways employees and the other groups of city employees. To this rivalry between the Catholic unions and the CCL was added a third element: another group of civil servants hoped to form a completely independent union without ties to any other organization. An arbitration board was formed to determine which of the three groups was the most representative. The Catholic union won out, and the others rallied to it as they had promised to do. But the steering committee of the Catholic union was reorganized to permit the integration of elements from the two other groups. Three representatives of each tendency were elected to form "the committee of nine". When the City refused to recognize the union, it was this committee which unleashed and directed the strike movement.

On December 16 the civil servants' assembly had given the committee of nine a mandate to demand that the city recognize the union and immediately grant improved salaries and working conditions. On Saturday the 18th the committee made representations to the president of the Québec Municipal Affairs Commission, Mr. L.-E. Potvin, and gave him an ultimatum: the union wanted an answer before five o'clock in the afternoon on Monday the 20th. When the deadline arrived no answer had been given, and the committee of nine, after holding an emergency meeting, called a new general assembly of the civil servants.

At the Monday night assembly attended by about half of the two thousand civil servants, as well as by top leaders of the Canadian and Catholic Confederation of Labour and two provincial legislators, Messrs. Joseph Francoeur and Georges Caron, the union members were invited to vote by secret ballot on the action to be taken. There were 927 votes in favour of the strike, 40 votes against, and four spoiled ballots.

The municipal authorities, warned in the evening of the union's decision, conferred for part of the night. The President of the Executive Committee, Mr. J.-O. Asselin, at first decided to close City Hall, but some service chiefs assured him that hundreds of civil servants would be at their posts the next day. These service chiefs were wrong. The next day only about ten young civil servants could be found at City Hall, going from room to room turning off the lights. When Mr. Asselin asked them why, they explained that they wanted to save the City money by preventing useless expenditure on electricity.

The municipal politicians, only too happy to embarrass the provincial government that was keeping them under trusteeship, showed themselves to be very sympathetic to the strikers.

The President of the Executive Committee, Mr. Asselin, declared on the first day that the municipal administration was powerless to settle labour conflicts in its current dependent state. He added that the civil servants' strike was a direct consequence "of the weakness shown a few days ago in the strike by the policemen, the firemen and the public works employees". Another man seemed to be of this opinion: Mr. Honoré Parent, who had been Québec's delegate to the city for more than three years, had resigned after the strike on the 14th, when he realized that there was going to be another work stoppage on his hands.

The Mayor of Montréal, Adhémar Raynault, visited the strikers late in the morning on December 21. "I have no scruples about meeting you," he told them. "You deserve sincere congratulations for the tact which you have shown since the beginning of the strike. It will always give me pleasure to meet with members of movements like yours.

"I must tell you that I cannot do or say anything. I can, however, affirm that I am in favour of better treatment for all you civil servants... You are excellent propagandists for the cause of just and reasonable salaries for Québec workers."

A city councillor, Jean-Marie Savignac, also expressed his sympathy with the strikers, and made an indirect attack against the federal government, which he accused of accumulating surpluses, thanks to the war effort, without letting the other levels of government profit from them. "It's unfair," he said, "because the cost of living is increasing for everybody. I can tell you that the members of the Municipal Affairs Commission receive (cost-of-living) indemnities of $50 per week, while you civil servants only get $1.98 per week. In Verdun, a city which depends on Montréal, the workers receive $4.60, or the full indemnity."

And Mr. Savignac issued a warning to those who might want to put the burden of improved conditions for the civil servants on the proprietors of Montréal: "I firmly assure the proprietors that the (municipal) council will not vote in favour of the increase in the property tax. Let Québec, which put us in this scrape, set this whole question to rights."

Nonetheless, to tell the truth, few people seemed to be moved by the civil servants' strike. According to Mr. Gérard Picard who was leading the strike as Secretary General of the CCCL, "The public did not feel endangered in the case of the municipal civil servants. For example, if you close the finance service at City Hall, the tax payers are not annoyed at all; they don't have to pay their taxes. But if you shut down the fire department, if you stop the police or the manual employees, the sewers and the public works, with all the side effects that come out of that, it's a little different."

The civil servants had very few trump cards in their hands to hasten the settlement of their conflict. They had believed that at least, with their absence, the other employees of the City would not be paid. But no, the City made agreements with the banks and the approximate salaries were paid, with an agreement that the necessary adjustments would be made when the clerks returned to work.

As another means of pressure, the civil servants had thought of closing the Meurling Refuge, a shelter for the homeless. At the request of the Archbishop of Montreal, Monseigneur Charbonneau, the strikers reversed that decision and left the Refuge open. In return the Archbishop, one week into the strike, made a substantial donation to the union to help the strikers hold out.

"I remember one afternoon," relates Mr. Roméo Éthier, who was treasurer of the union and a member of the committee of nine, "Mr. Bruneau (the president of the union) and I left our strike headquarters at Place Jacques-Cartier to go see Monseigneur Charbonneau... to ask him for financial help. He told us that he was going to think about it and that he would give us news. The two of us went back by bus and when we arrived at the door of our local at Place Jacques-Cartier there was a big black car at the door. We asked ourselves what was happening. We went into the local: it was Monseigneur Charbonneau who had gone upstairs with a cheque. He had just given us $1,500."

Mr. Éthier also solicited shopkeepers. "I can tell you," he recounts, "that we could have had all the money necessary to continue our strike for... there was no limit. A lawyer, a certain St. James Street lawyer... had offered us all the necessary financial support. He was a member of the Union Nationale, and since it was the Liberal Party that was in power... he wanted to play politics with that. At that time we refused completely."

All considered, the aid of the Archbishop was the most important. Monseigneur Charbonneau also intervened a little later on with the provincial government, to help settle the conflict. "Monseigneur Charbonneau," said Mr. Éthier, "was an impulsive man—I still see him then—when he saw that the bosses were getting too ambitious at the expense of the worker."

But despite the support from such an eminent source, the strike was a long one, 23 days in all. "And then I remember," said Mr. Éthier again, "Christmas Eve, Mr. Bruneau (the president of the union) told us at seven o'clock: 'Well then, boys, go home; we'll come back the day after Christmas; so Merry Christmas and go to midnight mass' — all that, eh. And at a quarter to eleven, I was taking my bath and the telephone rang—we were called to the strike headquarters at a quarter to eleven on Christmas Eve. I told my wife: 'Well, take off your dress and put on your nightgown; midnight mass will be for next year.' We had known that Mr. Asselin (president of the Executive Committee of the City) had proposals to make to us, that he wanted to settle it before the holiday period. It was a false rumour. So we went through periods like that. Naturally, we got tired."

If the union leaders were sometimes tired, the strikers also were becoming weary. Without a salary in the middle of a holiday period, having to go on picket duty in the cold of a Montréal December, worried about the lack of progress of their cause, certain strikers appeared to be very nervous. Some persons who had gone back to work were violently evicted from their offices. There was some muttering about plans to give a few key personages of the municipal administration a bad time, but these plans were never carried out.

On December 30, according to Mr. Éthier, the strikers "became cocky. We had a picket line that completely encircled City Hall, then I remember that we went to the Palais de Justice where it was known that Mr. Godbout (the Québec Premier) was. Notre Dame Street was blocked, black with people. I got up on one of the columns there, the big columns... the enthusiasm that I had... I asked Mr. Godbout to come out of there — it was known that he was in his office — to come out to negotiate with us, or let us go in to his office. Not all the people that were there, only two or three. The police arrived, and naturally they made us circulate..."

Even before this mass demonstration, internal tensions had agitated the strikers. Under pressure from discontented members, two successive votes were held to find out if the strike should be continued. On December 27, there were 411 persons who expressed their desire to continue, while 268 wanted to go back to work. On December 28, there were 762 votes to continue, 527 to end the strike.

Starting on the first day of 1944, the pressure on the provincial government sharpened. On January 5 the Premier and a few ministers met with a delegation from the union in Québec City. The meeting lasted several hours, and at six o'clock in the evening, according to Mr. Éthier, "Premier Godbout said: 'We're going to adjourn until eight o'clock.' We answered: 'No, this evening it is impossible, because we have been invited by the Québec civil servants to attend a little party, but we will come back tomorrow.' Then the Premier said: 'But tomorrow is Epiphany' (the feast of the Kings). And we said: 'The Kings or us, whatever you want; in this kind of situation, we can skip the Kings.' He (the Premier) hesitated; he hesitated, but in the end he had to agree to come sit with his Cabinet on Epiphany."

Four days later on January 10 the government of Québec proposed a settlement to the strikers: return to work, no discrimination against the union members, and arbitration of working conditions.

"We knew," explained Mr. Éthier, "that there was no other way out — just arbitration — since the strike couldn't last forever, because we didn't have the finances…" The union members expressed themselves in a new vote, and on January 13, after 23 days of strike, life resumes its normal course at Montréal City Hall.

The working conditions of the civil servants had to be submitted to the ruling of an arbitration board presided over by Mr. Théo Lespérance. The report, leading to the signing of the first contract, gave the civil servants a lump sum of $200, plus a salary increase of 10 per cent, payment of overtime, and shorter hours.

But the most extraordinary aspect was without a doubt the fact that the civil servants ended up getting a full salary for their 23 days on strike. Some of them had worked during the conflict, particularly a team which clandestinely transported the amusement tax tickets used by the theatres and other places of entertainment through a tunnel linking City Hall and police headquarters. The union based its decision on the City's promise not to discriminate between strikers and non-strikers, and pointed out that payments had been made to certain civil servants. It thus obtained an advantage which few strikers in history have enjoyed: the payment of a salary for time spent on strike.

epilogue

Who said that history is like a series of bridges that we build from ourselves to ourselves across chaos? There are all sorts of bridges—the majestic laceworks of steel and the little wooden bridges of the Québec countryside. There are also all sorts of historical works, and the present one is among the most modest. But through the narrow lens of some strikes which unfolded 30 or 40 years ago, an image came to me of what the decade in question was to Québec.

Myself and others of my generation have been made to believe that before we reached adulthood around 1960, there was nothing but darkness in Québec, a darkness that was barely brightened by a few great feats of arms like the strike of the asbestos miners in 1949 or that of the textile workers of Louiseville a few years later.

However, as the preceding pages testify, it was nothing like that. Not only did the Québécois workers know the meaning of fighting for their dignity and their bread, at least from the Thirties and even before, but organizations and institutions supported them that were no less Québécois for being neither nationalist nor Catholic.

And even among these nationalists, who were afterwards labelled to us as nothing but vile conservatives, there was, starting in the Thirties, a vigourous current which adopted as its own the labour struggle and the desire of the Québécois workers to have their legitimate place within society.

Let us just read the text of a speech made at Saint-Georges de Beauce on August 12, 1934, by Paul Gouin, founding leader of the Action Libérale Nationale, a speech reproduced in *Le Devoir* the next day. His remarks on the labour reforms preached by his party are revealing. He proposed, among other things, the adoption of a labour contract law, the revision of the minimum wage law, the institution of medicare (a measure which was not adopted in Québec until 1970), the regulation of price-fixing (a measure which is still not law as these lines are being written), the elimination of slums by encouraging the construction of housing for workers, and payment of just wages to workers to facilitate their acquisition of property.

A few years after the Action Libérale Nationale had been stabbed in the back by the conservative premier, Maurice Duplessis (who, however, had relied on it to take power), another political formation was born which was the spiritual heir of the ALN: the Bloc Populaire, created in 1942. The Bloc also proposed a war on "economic dictatorship and the adoption of labour laws which would strengthen the economic status of the worker."

Of course neither the ALN nor the Bloc took power. But each of them mobilized the energies of an important group of young Québécois. Perhaps for several, if not the majority of these militants, an opening to the labour world was replaced as a priority by nationalist preoccupations. But this opening was nevertheless clearly expressed. We have neither more nor less reason to doubt the sincerity of the men who inscribed this in their programmes than we have to doubt the convictions of those who, in 1949 or today, proclaimed and still proclaim their attachment to the labour cause.

And finally, it was Québécois voters in the Northwestern mining region of the province who sent a member of the social democratic party, the CCF, to the Québec Legislative Assembly in 1944. That this parliamentarian renounced his party afterwards does not mean that the workers who elected him had not known how to lend a deaf ear to the red-baiting of a certain type of clergy, and to give their adherence to the principles of democratic socialism.

Clearly the "opening to the left" in Québec did not begin just ten years ago, or even twenty years ago. And if one were to go back to the origins of Québec history, one would perhaps find a chain that was no less dynamic for being fragile and besieged, a chain of events of a radical character which would show a face of Québec different from the one that has been too easily accepted. One would be likely and even sure to find Québécois who were as ready as other North Americans to understand the meaning of industrial society and to fight to carve themselves a legitimate place in it. One would then perhaps less easily accept the thesis that Québec, before 1960 or thereabouts, was only a community of backward and diehard Catholic peasants.

Why does the collective memory of the Québécois seem not to have retained any events but those which led to defeat? The strike of the asbestos miners in 1949 and that of the copper miners of the Gaspé in 1957 were epics, and I agree that they deserve the place that they have taken in history. But they were also "lost" strikes. The strikes described in the preceding chapters, however, were almost all "won" strikes. Why have they been spoken of so little up to now? Are Québécois ashamed of remembering the good blows they have struck, just as the Puritans were ashamed of enjoying themselves?

Perhaps there has been too much reliance, in the examination of the social history of Québec, on the statements of official spokesmen, on those whom others have called "the situation definers". There should have been more attention paid to those who made this history, to whom even this book has not given all the place that was at first reserved for them.

appendix

the choice of conflicts and the framework of the study

If one only considers strikes which affected more than a thousand workers or involved more than a thousand working-days, a clear evolution of the labour movement in the period studied can be perceived.

In 1934 it was the garment industry in Montréal which was the theatre for four strikes of more than a thousand employees in Québec. Among the strikes of lesser scope but longer duration, there was that of the Noranda miners (see Chapter II), other strikes in the garment industry, a strike at a paper mill in Dolbeau in Lac-Saint-Jean, a furniture factory strike in Montréal, and, also in Montréal, a strike of radio musicians which was supported by radio musicians in other urban centres of Canada.

In 1953 the garment industry in Montréal was again the setting for two strikes involving more than 1,000 workers, while a third strike on this scale unfolded in a cotton mill in Trois-Rivières. Strikes of more than a thousand work-days affected the shoe industry in Montréal and Valley Junction, the fur industry in Saint-Jean, and the garment industry in Montréal.

In 1936 there were only two strikes in which a thousand workers or more participated: in the taxi industry in Montréal and in a cotton mill in Trois-Rivières. There were four strikes which occasioned time losses of more than a thousand work-days, of which two were in Montréal (leather and clothing), one in a saw-mill in Cabano, and one in a pottery factory in Saint-Jean.

The year 1937, with its 45 strikes, was a secondary peak, in this respect, in the decade studied. It was marked by strike movements in the textile industry and the shipyards[1], the garment industry in Montréal (see Chapter III), and the asbestos mines in Asbestos. It also experienced 15 strikes of more than a thousand workdays lost, affecting packinghouses in Montréal, a wool-processing plant in Saint-Jean (twice), the garment industry in Sorel, silk factories in Sherbrooke, Saint-Hyacinthe, Acton Vale, and Louiseville, cap-making and embroidery enterprises in Montréal, a dress factory in Montréal (Ideal Dress, which was not affected by the strike movement described in Chapter III), a paper mill in Trois-Rivières, a foundry in Sorel and a plumbing accessories business in Montréal.

From 1938 to 1940 there was only one strike affecting more than a thousand workers, that in the aluminum and construction industries in Arvida (see Chapter IV). But this was the year of the first strike in a rolling-mill, in Montréal (at Peck Rolling Mills, a setting for repeated incidents during the war), and the first strike in a steel mill, both organized by the CIO. There was also a strike in a woodworking business at Lac Mégantic, and a strike by highway labourers in Saint-Nicolas, near Québec City.

In 1942 the explosion came: strikes by more than a thousand workers in the tobacco industry in Montréal (July and September), in the shoe industry in Québec, in a sawmill in Rimouski, in a munitions factory in Chénier, in the shipyards of Sorel and Lauzon. Only in the last case was a union affiliated to the new CIO involved. The others were divided equally among unions affiliated to the AFL and Catholic unions.

As for strikes causing losses of more than a thousand work days, there were 22 of them that year, as many as the total number of strikes in 1940. Seven of these strikes hit the wood and paper industries; two, the shoe industry; two, the naval yards, and two, the textile industry. As for the others, they affected a bakery in Lasalle, a distillery in Lasalle, the Montréal cigar makers, a metallurgical business in Beauharnois, a cable factory in Saint-Jean, a steel mill at Longue Pointe, a limestone furnace in Joliette, and a group of bank clerks in Montréal.

Of these 22 strikes, twelve were led by unions affiliated with the AFL, those supposedly "old" unions from whom vigorous action was no longer expected. Five were led by unions affiliated to the CIO or to the CCL, and four were organized by Catholic unions. In one case, the archives do not indicate the union affiliation.

The following year, 1943, strikes were less numerous but, on the whole, more spectacular. There are records of thirteen affecting more than a thousand workers, among them those in the pulp and paper industry in Lac-Saint-Jean and those in the public services in Montréal (see Chapters IV, V and VI). There was also an important strike movement in the naval yards, in June and July, in Montréal, Québec, Lauzon and Sorel, and in which were involved both the craft unions affiliated to the AFL and the industrial unions of the CIO and the CCL. The Montréal machinists went on strike in June, the workers in the Angus shops—where the rolling stock of the Canadian Pacific Railways was manufactured—stopped work for six days in July; an important airplane factory in Montréal was paralyzed in August, and the aluminum plant in Shawinigan was hit in October.

There were also seventeen strikes involving losses of more than a thousand work-days during the same year. The strike of the asbestos miners, started the previous year, continued in East Broughton. Shoe manufacturing enterprises in Montréal, Québec and Acton Vale were immobilized for a long time. Conflicts affected textile enterprises in Québec City suburbs, in Farnham and in Granby. There were also long strikes in the fur and garment industries in Québec City, in the paper industry in Dolbeau, at Lac Saint Jean (see Chapter IV), in a copper refinery, a glass works and stuffing plants in Montréal, and in a foundry in Hull. There were, finally, several strikes in the munitions factory in Chénier which had also been hit the year before.

Then, in 1944, there was a sort of truce. Three full-scale strikes took place in the rubber plants of Saint-Jérôme, the men's garment industry and the tramways in Montréal. Four strikes causing time losses of more than a thousand work-days took place: in the rubber industry in Montréal, in a paper mill in Saint-Jean, in a foundry in l'Islet, and in the naval yards in Montréal. It was a peaceful year, compared to the two previous years.

A selection had to be made out of this considerable mass of large-scale strikes of ten conflicts for detailed description, based both on interviews with participants (each time "witnesses" are mentioned in this work, it means persons who made themselves available to be interviewed) and on the written documents: reports of commissions of inquiry, accounts from the general press and the union press.

The strikes which had already been the objects of historical works, such as the strikes in the asbestos mines[2], at Dominion Textile and in the naval yards of Sorel[3], were eliminated, because it seemed futile at this time to duplicate work that had already been done.

Then, the strikes which were part of a movement going beyond the geographical boundaries of Québec (e.g. those of the seamen and the packers), were eliminated, because to include them, it would have been necessary to alter the scope of a work of research centered on Québec.

The only strikes retained among those remaining were strikes which affected at least 500 workers and caused the loss of at least a thousand work-days.

There again it was necessary to make a choice. The criteria which prevailed in the selection of the dozen strikes studied in the preceding chapters were inspired by a desire to give the most varied possible sampling of the conflicts of the period.

The first criterion touches on industrial or employment sectors. Thus, given the importance of the textile and clothing industries in the Québec economy of the

Thirties, it seemed indispensible to describe strikes in this sector. This was done in Chapter III. Similarly the mining, wood and aluminum industries commended special attention. Finally, events in the public sector were kept (Chapters V and VI) not only because of the importance that public employment had and still has for Francophone Québécois, but also because strikes in this sector during the war offer an unpublished and spectacular dimension of conflict.

The second criterion was geographical location. It was necessary to confine myself to conflicts which unfolded in the metropolis, Montréal, as well as to those in the mining regions of the north west (Noranda) or in average-sized and peripheral towns like those of Lac-Saint-Jean. At the beginning I also hoped to deal with strikes in the region of the provincial capital, Québec, and specifically with the strikes in the naval yards, but the research had to be interrupted before the necessary data on these strikes had been collected. Likewise, I planned to describe the history of repeated strikes in a small-town enterprise in the heart of Québec, more specifically, at Franco-Canadian Dyeing in Saint-Jean, where there were three strikes during the Thirties and Forties, the third ending with the closing of the factory. There again, the research was not completed.

The third criterion concerns the evolution of union institutions. This involved studying militant but defunct organizations like the Workers' Unity League (Chapters II and III) as well as the first incursions into Québec by the Congress of Industrial Organizations (Chapter III), and the evolution of the Catholic unions and of the Canadian Congress of Labour, with the struggles which opposed both of them to the unions of the American Federation of Labour and of the Trades and Labour Congress of Canada (Chapters IV to VI). In this respect there is a gap in the present study: I do not describe any strike where the AFL or TLC unions adopted a militant and aggressive attitude, although there had been some — by the airplane and tobacco workers, for example.

Finally, I looked for strikes which illustrated or seemed to have influenced government intervention, whether it was as a last gasp of the Liberal regime of Alexandre Taschereau, or in the first hours of the conservative Union Nationale government of Maurice Duplessis, or in the form of the diverse federal and provincial wartime interventions which led in 1944 to new legislation. It is by virtue of this criterion, for example, that the strikes described in Chapter IV were retained, even if in this case, and in this case alone, there were no interviews with participants to complement the written sources like the reports of government inquiries and the newspaper accounts. The aluminum and pulp and paper strikes in the Lac-Saint-Jean region all had a direct link with the government labour policy; in the first case, it is the federal policy with regard to conflicts in war industries which is involved; in the second case, the whole question of criteria for union representativeness was studied after these strikes, leading government investigators to conclusions which necessarily exercised a determining influence on the legislation.

Once having selected the twelve strikes described in this book, it was necessary to establish a frame of reference so as not to sail off course, to use a navigators' expression, nor to risk neglecting some important aspect of those conflicts I retained for fuller study.

It is here that the sociological works dealing with strikes and social conflicts come in. There are not very many of these works and their quality, on the whole, is even less impressive. However, when one begins to perceive the complexity and the richness of the strike seen as a social phenomenon, one becomes more indulgent towards authors who have tried to encompass it either by adopting the microscopic approach of entomologists, or by applying themselves to great frescoes that are spectacular rather than precise. It is as if a strike makes a vertical cut through the superimposed layers of economic and social life, laying bare, sometimes by caricature or distortion, the diversified network of relations which make up the fabric of a society.

In the face of this phenomenon, the observer, whether a historian, economist, sociologist or journalist, cannot pretend to be truly impartial, since he is part of the society that the strike puts into question. The authors consulted in relation to this study all betray the nature of their own political and social options, even when they proclaim the strictest neutrality.[4]

Works which are solely chronicles of particular strikes are not at issue here. Among the books consulted three categories, or three tendencies, can be distinguished. There are first of all those who limit their analysis to the enterprise, considering it as an isolated unit. Then there are those who broaden their frontiers to take account of the totality of labour relations in a given society, handling them either from an economic or a sociological point of view. Finally, there is a work which could be described as macro-sociology, or political theory, which describes strikes within the evolution of society as a whole, politics being tacitly defined here as conflict management.

The first approach is microscopic, entomological.[5] It seems to take it for granted that an enterprise is a closed universe, which is self-sufficient and which can be studied without referring to the larger society of which it is a part.

Thus Gouldner explains the strike that he examines by the fact that in the firm it affects, an administrator of the traditional and "paternal" type has been replaced by an administrator of the bureaucratic, and thus more impersonal, type. Sayles analyzes the relative propensity to conflict of different divisions within a firm by dealing with the status of the craft bodies in relation to each other. Paterson and Willet push what could be described as formalism a notch further by dwelling on the spatial distribution of the various actors at the outbreak of a spontaneous strike.

Considerations of this nature can be useful, particularly to personnel directors or union leaders. More particularly, however, in the case of the last authors cited, they lend themselves better to strike analyses done on the spot than to historical reconstructions.

Nevertheless, they were useful in the formation of a frame of reference for this study. Thus, I took into account the types of occupations in a firm—it is not inconsequential, for example, that the aluminum strike started among the vat workers, or that unionism among policemen first affected the motorcycle cops. The interpersonal relations within a firm were also examined, and in using Gouldner's approach, it is worth noting that the strikes by the Montréal city employees came about at a time when more coldly impersonal relations had replaced the informal relations born out of political favouritism, following the intervention of the provincial government in the affairs of the city and the nomination of an administrator delegated by Québec.

As for the second approach revealed in the books consulted, the one that links a particular strike to the total labour relations picture in a society, there is first of all a subcategory of authors whose main preoccupation is with economics. [6]

Their approach makes wide use of statistical data, while in this study statistics are hardly used. Thus, Kerr and Siegel believe that workers are especially inclined to strike when a lot of them find themselves doing "unpleasant" tasks and being cut off from the other workers. For his part, Rees discovered, in studying the period from 1915 to 1948, that strikes follow the curve of economic cycles faithfully enough between 1915 and 1938, but break away from it between 1939 and 1948; he explains this change by saying that state intervention and its various consequences began to change the rules of the game in 1938. Weintraub, a student of the period from 1949 to 1961, rediscovers a correspondence between economic cycles and strikes, the crest of the wave of cycles slightly preceding that of the strikes. Knowles, finally, in his analyses takes into account the importance that a particular industry has at a given historical moment in the economy of a region or of a country.

As has been pointed out above, this particular study does not permit statistical analysis, and there could thus be no question of testing the hypotheses of the authors cited. Certain data can however be retained as indicative. For example, the garment strikes discussed in Chapter III took place, in the first part of the period examined, during years when total employment in the textiles sector was reaching a peak: in 1934 the number of wage workers in the sector rose by more than ten per cent compared to 1933; in 1937, the year of the second major conflict, employment in the same category rose by about eight per cent compared to the previous year. For each of the years in question, the fluctuations in the total number of jobs for the wage workers follow the same curve, except that the variations are even more important for the total than for the textile sector.

Moreover the years 1942 and 1943, or those in which the strikes were most numerous both in absolute terms and in terms of scope and duration, were also peak years for employment in the manufacturing sector. In 1941 the total number of wage workers in all industrial sectors was 276,415. The following year, it climbed to 342,405; in 1943 it went up to 374,605, falling back to 360,965 in 1944.

Books analyzing the relations between strikes and the total labour picture from an economic perspective require rigourous statistical returns for verification, but books handling the same problem within a sociological perspective rely more on impressionist adaptations.

Among this new category of works offered by the sociologists[7], the study by Bendix presents particularly attractive hypotheses. He does a comparative study of the evolution of management ideologies in the Anglo-Saxon world and in Russia, and demonstrates how the perception of the foundations for and acceptable exercise of legitimate social power, which is transmitted by the tradition of a society, influences the conception of authority held by members of the same society.

It would be interesting to examine the ties between the traditional forms of power in Québec, notably ecclesiastical power, and the forms of authority which have been or still are accepted in Québec firms. One could also ask oneself if Québec greatly differs in this regard from the North American pattern. I could not avoid wondering for example, why the major strikes at the beginning of the period I examined were started and led by groups ethnically and sometimes religiously different from the mass of Catholic and French-speaking Québécois. The conciliatory role played by the leaders of the Catholic unions also deserves to be examined. Despite the fact that French-speaking Québécois were Catholics and submissive to religious authority, they still participated in radical movements and in epic strikes. The popular hypothesis that Québécois workers were little more than docile sheep before the famous strike by the asbestos miners in 1949, perhaps will not hold out long against an examination of the facts that is more rigourous than the analyses that we have been offered up to now. Remember that the working girls of 1937 were also Québécoises!

The study by Touraine offers another method of interpreting the evolution of labour relations in a society, considered this time from the standpoint of the labour organizations. He distinguishes the "revolutionary" period, when the unions are excluded from power, from a second period when they participate in power without holding power, and finally from a final stage, experienced by the newly independent countries, when the unions are "in power".

If one accepts the status given to unions by legislation as a measure of union power, one can say that at the beginning of the period studied, Québec unions were at the first stage described by Touraine, while in 1944 — with the proclamation of laws forcing the employers to negotiate with the unions representative of their employees — they entered the second. The period thus would be an important turning point.

Touraine also classifies the levels challenged by labour action: a political level for the redistribution of social power, an economic level for a redistribution of goods, and a level that he calls "the labour revolt", directly ties to the conditions of production, a revolt which rejects the constraints both of work and of the technical organization of work, on the shop floor even more than on the company level.

Among the strikes described in the chapters of this study, the "labour revolt" is most apparent in the strikes by the workers, especially the women workers, in the women's clothing industry, and all the evidence points to the conclusion that the main advantage that the women workers finally obtained was greater justice in the distribution of employment and a greater respect for their persons. There is no doubt that a replica of the mediaeval "droit de seigneur" existed in the garment industry less than forty years ago, where women's bodies were exploited to an extent not found in other industries.

In the other strikes examined, the three types of objectives dealt with by Touraine intersect and intermingle with each other. The accent put on any particular objective seems to be more applicable to factors external to the firms than to their internal operation, or to the specific interpretations offered by the unions involved.

For outside of the particular contours of a given conflict, there are roles and attitudes which are shared, in different degrees, by all the workers on the one hand, and all the employers on the other, within a society. Kornhauser, Dubin and Ross stress that the conception each party in a labour dispute has of its adversary's interests is more important than the "economic facts". The authors attribute different "ethical foundations" to the positions of the employers and the unions. The former, they say, postulate the primacy of the value of private enterprise, and as a corollory of this, the importance of the material welfare of individuals. The latter see themselves as the defenders of social justice, and as the protectors of the worker against exploitation and the degradation which his employee status imposes on him.

Katz develops this theme of the irreducible opposition of employers and unions. He rejects the viewpoint that industrial conflict can be eliminated by concessions made in a climate of peace. How would that be possible, he says, when the management role of a firm

141

requires adherence to the objectives of productivity and profit rather than to the satisfying of the various needs of the workers. And even without this conflict between objectives, the workers and their unions will inevitably and always seek to snatch new advantages — "new aspirations and needs will constantly go beyond what has already been obtained."

The editors of *Industrial Conflict* and Daniel Katz perhaps push their fatalistic view of the inevitable character of labour conflicts too far. Perhaps they do it in reaction to so many American industrial relations specialists, in whose eyes definitive peace always seems to be possible and imminent. But their hypotheses do not seem to adapt well to particular industrial sectors, and still less to enterprises or groups of enterprises. In the dress industry, for example, after a period of lively agitation, there was not a single open conflict for the thirty years between 1940 and 1970.

The analyses which conclude that social conflict is permanent seem more suitable when one no longer keeps to one enterprise, one industry, or even to all of the employers and unionized workers, but rather looks at the social system as a whole. Sellier in particular does this.[8] He sees the strike not as a phenomenon which arises solely from the technique of industrial relations, but as a "rupture of the social balance", and this balance not only involves bosses and workers, but a whole network of relations between these and the other social forces on which they depend, including the state. The strike, "a contestation of the power of the employer and an expression of the power of the salary earners" imposes itself "not only on the employer but on all of the society by which he holds his power."

The power of each of the parties in a strike, according to Sellier, is affected by the relations of these parties with other members and groups of the society, whether they be the political parties, the press, the Church, the other popular organisms, or whatever. Thus it is not necessary to talk about the style of management native to a particular enterprise. It is readily understandable that a miners' strike involving men "foreign" to the majority in origin and language, and led by a union suspected of hostility to the very foundations of a society, will be less likely to end in success for the strikers than another strike led, for example, by members of the majority ethnic, linguistic and religious group, identified with the type of unionism that is most acceptable to this majority — Catholic unionism — and opposing French-Canadian workers to an English-speaking management and to a federal government identified as the promoter of a war to which an important segment of opinion is vigourously opposed.

On the basis of these books, and on the basis of ideas I derived during the years when I closely followed many strikes as a labour reporter for a daily newspaper, I worked out a sort of grid which I used as a frame of reference for the examination of the strikes described in these chapters.

This grid would have the graphic form of three concentric circles, defining the frontiers of the phenomenon studied. In the centre would be the firm, the nucleus of the subject. This is surrounded by a circle with a larger diameter circumscribing the geographic region where the enterprise is situated, and the second circle is itself encircled by a third, indicating the country or, in this case, the province of Québec.

From the centre of the smallest circle to the periphery of the largest, the model is cut in slices (yes, like a pie!) which correspond to the various factors which, in my opinion, have to be taken into account in the examination of every strike: workers, employers, industrial structure, economic fluctuations, management and union ideologies, governments and parties, ethnic groups, Churches, public opinion. One has to look for the manifestation of the impact of these diverse factors in each of the three circles, that is to say, at the level of the enterprise as much as at the level of the region and of the country. To avoid losing oneself in the whirlpool of reports and events which overlap each other and correspond in any strike that has any scope, everything starts from the centre — the enterprise or the group of enterprises — and the events are described in chronological order.

It should not be necessary to make it clear that I do not pretend to offer a schema for the interpretation of strikes that can compare with those that more knowledgeable authors have worked out. I simply want to indicate to the reader the guidelines I have used in doing this work.

The schema described above was the basis of the questionnaire answered by those witness-participants in the described strikes who could be found and who agreed to be interviewed. Each interview lasted at least an hour and often much longer. [9]

FOOTNOTES:

1. Cf. *En grève,* op. cit.

2. Cf EN COLLABORATION, under the direction of PIERRE ELLIOTT TRUDEAU, *La grève de l'amiante,* Les éditions Cité Libre, 1956.

3. *En grève,* op. cit.

4. I would not know how to be an exception to this rule, and I freely admit that in the event of a strike, I am more readily sympathetic to the worker than to the employer or even the union. Among the unions, I prefer the more dynamic to the more conservative, and the grass roots militants to the leaders roosting on the summit.

5. Cf. A.W. GOULDNER, *Wildcat Strike,* Antioch Press, 1954; LEONARD SAYLES, *The Behavior of Industrial Work Groups,* John Wiley & Sons, 1958, and T.T. PATERSON & F.J. WILLET, "Unofficial Strike", in *The Sociological Review,* Vol. XLIII, section four, pp. 57-94, 1951.

6. KERR and SIEGEL, "The Interindustry Propensity to Strike", in KRONHAUSER, DUBIN & ROSS, editors, *Industrial Conflict,* McGraw Hill, 1954; ALBERT REES, "Industrial Conflict and Business Fluctuations", *Industrial Conflict,* idem.; ANDREW R. WEINTRAUB, "Prosperity versus Strikes: An Empirical approach", *Industrial and Labor Relations Review,* Vol. 19, no. 2, January 1966; KNOWLES, *Strikes, a Study of Industrial Conflict,* Oxford, 1952.

7. R. BENDIX, *Work and Authority in Industry: Ideologies of Management in the Course of Industrialization,* Harper Torchbooks, 1963; A. TOURAINE, "Contribution à la sociologie du mouvement ouvrier. Le syndicalisme de contrôle", *Cahiers Internationaux de Sociologie,* Vol. XXVIII, 1960, pp. 57-58; and in *Industrial Conflict* (loc. cit.), the editors' introduction (pp. 3-22) as well as DANIEL KATZ, "Satisfactions and Deprivations in Industrial Life", pp. 86-106.

8. FRANÇOIS SELLIER, *Stratégie de la lutte sociale,* Editions ouvrières, Paris, 1961. See especially Chapter XVII, "Les grèves", pp. 291-309.

9. Here is the profile of the questionnaire: 1) Biography of the interviewee; geographic and ethnic origin, religious affiliation, level of eduction, father's

occupation, age at time of conflict. 2) Working conditions before the conflict. 3) Immediate cause or pretext for the unleashing of the conflict. 4) The organizations in the dispute: a) on the workers' side, the union and its affiliation, the local, regional, provincial, national or international leadership; b) on the employer's side: isolated enterprise or part of a complex; proprietors or administrators; those in charge of negotiations and management; relations with other employers or management associations. 5) Evolution of the conflict; negotiations if they take place; violence; interventions by the police; strike breakers; duration; settlement. 6) The social context: ethnic and/or social origins of the protagonists; attitudes in the local community (shopkeepers, Church, liberal professions, municipal politicians, local press); relations if any with a wider community. 7) The return to work: conditions, climate, impact.

QUEBEC AND RADICAL SOCIAL CHANGE

edited by Dimitrios Roussopoulos

This collection of essays drawn from the Canadian quarterly journal, OUR GENERATION which was founded in 1961 covers a wide range of social questions. The journal is well-known for its outstanding contribution to the publication of important material on the evolution of Québec society. These essays have not appeared elsewhere in English when published over the years in the journal, and are brought all together in this volume for the first time.

The essays deal with nationalism, the role of intellectuals in society, the trade union movement, an analysis of various important elections, the contribution of students and youth, the question of class, and related questions.

Among the contributors are included: Marcel Rioux, Hélène David, Louis Maheu, Adèle Lauzon, Robert Favreau, Mario Dumais, Serge Carlos, Jean Laliberté, and others.

225 pages / Hardcover $10.95 / Paperback $3.95
ISBN 0-919618-52-9/ISBN: 09-919618-51-0
Contains: Canadian Shared Cataloguing in Publication Data

BLACK ROSE BOOKS No. E 17

DEMOCRACY
AND THE
WORK PLACE

by Harold B. Wilson

"A book which might conceivably be the most useful single volume ever produced for the modern socialists of Canada."

— Douglas Fisher, *Toronto Sun*

"Another recent book that should be read... Wilson provides the Canadian orientation... but he also goes beyond the philosophical approach to show how industrial democracy can be achieved..."

— Ed Finn, *Toronto Daily Star*

"Even though they might not like what they read, corporation managers should run out and buy a copy. They might then be partially prepared if the socialist hordes break down the door."

— George Dobie, *Vancouver Sun*

"...It may well become a classic of socialist literature."

— Roy LaBerge, *The Courier*

"We have been waiting for a long time for a book which deals constructively with the world of work which most Canadians experience in their daily life. For Canadians this has been a neglected subject. Harold Wilson's book is an important exception. It is timely, relevant and controversial."

— Gerry Hunnius, Atkinson College, York University

267 pages / Hardcover $10.95 / Paperback $3.95
ISBN: 0-919618-23-5 / ISBN: 0-919618-22-7

BLACK ROSE BOOKS No. C15

MOTHER WAS
NOT A PERSON

edited by
Margret Andersen

This book is an anthology of writings by Montréal women. It deals with the politics, poetry, educational and related dimensions of women in our society. It is mandatory reading for the general public in Canada, as we are flooded with books on women from the USA.

"Many of the writings in this anthology warrant an in-depth study; many, because of their literary quality, provide reading pleasure. A diversified compilation, **Mother** should be read by all those interested in the feminist movement and especially by those curious to know of the specifics concerning the movement in Québec. Teachers wishing to incorporate into their civilization courses the history and evolution of the women's movement in the francophonic world will find this Canadian publication a valuable source of information."

Prof. Anthony Caprio,
Lehman College, SUNY.

Contributors to *Mother Was Not A Person* include Marlene Dixon, Lise Fortier, Katherine Walters, Christine Garside, Lilian Reinblatt, Mary Melfi and Lucia Kowaluk.

2nd Edition-
274 pages / Hardcover $10.95 / Paperback $3.95
ISBN; 0-919618-12-X / ISBN: 0-919618-00-6

BLACK ROSE BOOKS No. D7

WALLS AND BARS

BY EUGENE V. DEBS

Debs went to jail for the Pullman boycott in '94 and ran for President of the United States from Atlanta Penitentiary in 1920.

His socialist indictment of jails is brought to date by labour leader Patrick Gorman' 1973 Introduction.

Prof. Bernard Brommel adds the most extensive Debs bibliography yet published.

039/288 pages/Paperback $4.50/$8.95 Hardcover

THE PULLMAN STRIKE

BY WILLIAM H. CARWARDINE

This factual report of life and labour in the USA's most notorious company town during the 1894 strike has gone through several editions. Dr. Virgil Vogel has supplemented the reprint with a concise summary of the strike, the story of the American Railway Union, the arrest and conviction of Gene Debs for the Union's boycott of Pullman cars, and the far-reaching consequences of this pivotal episode in the history of American labour.

038/192 pages/Paperback $3.95/$8.95 Hardcover

THE AUTOBIOGRAPHY OF MOTHER JONES

EDITED BY MARY F. PARTON
Forward by Clarence Darrow

Born 1830, she mothered union struggles from 1871 to 1921, drilled strikers' wives to chase out gunmen and scabs. This new edition documents her amazing story.

"For half a century she appeared wherever labour troubles were acute, a little old woman... with shrewd, kindly gray eyes."

— *Dictionary of American Biography*

032/242 pages/ISBN 0-88286-001-1/Hardcover $8.50
Paperback $4.50

IMAGINATION IN POWER
The Occupation of Factories in France in 1968

BY ANDREE HOYLES

Shortly after the 1968 General Strike in France, Andrée Hoyles undertook a detailed survey of the factory occupations which were a crucial component in that dramatic upheaval. She interviewed numerous trade union officials and activists, conducted a detailed questionnaire and made an exhaustive study of material written in the course of the struggle.

026/72 pages/SBN 85124 058 5
Hardcover $4.50

CAN THE WORKERS RUN INDUSTRY?
KEN COATES, EDITOR

Who controls the economy? What are the levers for change? Conditions and plans in specific industries. What is the way forward? These are some of the notions examined by the contributors of this excellent paperback. Set in the context of the British economy which is staggering from one crisis to another, the issue of industrial democracy looms great. The aim of this book is to show that the best cure is to involve the workers actively and vitally in the process of making decisions. In this volume, trade union leaders, shop stewards, university teachers and political leaders present their views and their plans for the future.

020/250 pages   Paperback $2.45

THE BOLSHEVIKS AND WORKERS' CONTROL 1917-21

BY MAURICE BRINTON

Workers' control is again widely discussed and widely researched. This book has two aims. It seeks to contribute new factual material to the current discussion on workers' control. And it attempts a new kind of analysis of the fate of the Russian Revolution. The two objectives, as will be shown, are inter-related.

An impressive array of documentation is brought to bear on how the Bolshevik State related to the whole question of self-management in revolutionary Russia. Sources are used which have never before been so inter-related and interpreted within such a profound analysis. This book has great significance today especially for those who are interested in a historical understanding of the question of a democracy of participation and popular control.

02/100 pages Paperback $1.95/Hardcover $8.95

READINGS IN AMERICAN IMPERIALISM

EDITED BY K.T. FANN & DONALD C. HODGES

America's increasing involvement in the affairs of other countries has led many to question her motivations and purposes in defending interests abroad. This selection of essays examines the theory of imperialism inherent in capitalism, and discusses American economic and political involvement in South America, and its effects on Third World countries. Also discussed is the reaction to and effects of U.S. imperialism in the home country, and reactions of Third World spokesmen. Articles by Theodore Dos Santos, Conor Cruise O'Brien, Paul Baran, Harry Magdoff, Paul Sweezy, Fidel Castro, Lin Pao, and Che Guevara, among others, provide a comprehensive view of what many consider a basic policy inherent in this kind of social and economic structure which is antithetical to worldwide cooperation and human development.

06/384 pages/paperback $5.95/$9.95 hardcover
Extending Horizons Series

FROM LABOURISM TO SOCIALISM

The Political Economy of Labour in the 1970's
BY MICHAEL BARRAT BROWN

The new industrial revolution, the nature and implications of which are studied here in detail, creates both the necessity and the opportunity for an advance towards socialism. This is on the agenda for the 1970s; and presents the greatest challenge for the British Labour Movement. The book argues that a Party committed to social ownership and control and based on the Trade Union Movement, as the Labour Party is, can, with the extension of internal democracy, become an instrument for radical social change. But this, the author insists, implies the pressing of every reform with the fully mobilised power of the people right up to and beyond the limits imposed by capitalism. This book demonstrates how all the predictions of Crosland's "The Future of Socialism" which so influenced the Labour Party have proved erroneous. Now his critics must be heard.

018/265 pages   Hardcover: $10.00

SOCIALISM AND THE ENVIRONMENT

MALCOLM CALDWELL, KEN COATES,
ROBERT JUNGK, K.W. KAPP and
COLIN STONEMAN

Socialists need to elaborate an aggressive strategy, calculated to present the bills for the damage and waste of capitalism to those who have incurred them, and to prepare the ground for an alternative society. It is perfectly clear however that the struggle against pollution, the problems raised by ecologists combine to challenge not only the performance of our given economic system, but also the traditional socialist critique of that system.

019/200 pages   Hardcover: $6.50

MARX AND KEYNES:

THE LIMITS OF THE MIXED ECONOMY
BY PAUL MATTICK

The Keynesian hypothesis presumes to answer contemporary needs for a more stable and more extended economic structure. Mattick weighs these resources and materials against Marx's prediction of the inherent decline and collapse of capitalism, and views Keynes' mixed economy as a temporary system incapable of solving the inherent difficulties of capitalism. His work deals with all the significant problems of political economy: capital formation, credit, foreign trade, imperialism, and neo-colonialism. The author's sure grasp of both Marxist and Keynesian theory allows a clear and incisive exposition of their common features and divergences as well as their relevance to historical and contemporary outlines of the political economy.

04/364 pages/hardcover $8.95/paperback $4.95
Extending Horizons Series

PRINTED BY
LES ÉDITIONS MARQUIS LTÉE
MONTMAGNY